fuse / fracture
(poems 2001-2021)

Patrick Jones is author of six plays, three spoken word albums, nine books of poetry and lyricist on the *Even in Exile* album (James Dean Bradfield). He is currently Writer in Residence with The Royal College of Psychiatrists in Wales and adapting his 2016 play, *Before I Leave*, into a film. He was born in Tredegar, Wales. He has four children and two cats and lives at the foot of a mountain.

www.patrick-jones.info

fuse / fracture
(poems 2001-2021)

Patrick Jones

Foreword by James Dean Bradfield

PARTHIAN

Parthian, Cardigan SA43 1ED www.parthianbooks.com
First published in 2021
© Patrick Jones 2021
ISBN 978-1-913640-42-2
Editor: Susie Wildsmith
Cover image by Lucy Jane Frank Purrington
Cover design by Syncopated Pandemonium
Typeset by Elaine Sharples
Printed and bound by 4edge Limited, UK
Published with the financial support of the Welsh Books Council
British Library Cataloguing in Publication Data
A cataloguing record for this book is available from the British Library.

These words are dedicated to the loving memory of my mother and father, Irene and Allen and to the hope-filled dreams of my children: Elian, Evan, Ethan and Rebekah

Llyfrau. Gwybodaeth. Rhyfeddod

…it does not matter
to be one more stone, the dark stone,
the pure stone which the river bears away.
– Pablo Neruda

Whoever you are, no matter how lonely,
the world offers itself to your imagination,
– Mary Oliver

Contents

from THE GUERILLA TAPESTRY (1995)

from THE PROTEST OF DISCIPLINE (1996)

from MUTE COMMUNION (1997)

from FUSE (2001)

from AGAINST (2003)

from DARKNESS IS WHERE THE STARS ARE (2008)

from THE ASPIRATIONS OF POVERTY (2017)

from MY BRIGHT SHADOW (2020)

from EVEN IN EXILE (2020)

Foreword

I remember when I first read the lines

Wishing summer never came,
wishing everything could be the same

in 2001. They affected me in such a personal way, and then I realised that the lines were for me and my family. But the dedication had no significance really, did it? The poem had made its connection prior to my realisation.

Twenty years on and the new poems in this reissue bury even deeper into my senses, 'You', with the lines –

As life threw its lances
Its other
Possible smotherings
You were prepared
For the failing light.

'Residual' and 'Mornings Teach Us Shadows' are probably my favourite that he has ever written. Personal experience distilled, raw, visceral that aims to connect not confuse. I hope you feel the same way.

His past work still speaks to the present; 'The Guerilla Tapestry' which dates back to around 1995, still a protest song not yet finished, waiting to be primed for a new generation.

'Carelines' documents the presence in absences and reanimates isolation and suffering, yet makes it seem bearable. Isn't that what we always want from poetry?

James Dean Bradfield, 2021

New Poems

(2021)

Marcescence On A Spring Day

I have been driving around
For a week
With a black bag
Full of my mother's clothes

This is not easy
I cradle it in the boot
Like precious cargo
Afraid to
Dislodge the folded garments'
Perfect symmetry
Measurements of an interrupted life

At times I almost stop
At the charity shop
But I find myself unable to let go
Of the creases
Feeling the fabric
Between my fingers
As if a blanket
Of sanctuary
As a child
I'd hide behind
My mother's skirt
Not willing to
Go to school,
Most days,
She walked me back to the comfort of home
For now,
I will do the same,

Tr(Us)t

The delicately spun
Web
Between two people
Spoken silk
Scavenged from such sadness
Intrinsically woven
Into arteries
And neural pathways
From reached out fingertips
And the stoic routines of
Everyday
Fused from the fractures
Inherent in difference
Held together
Taut as a diving bungee
Measured
Never
To hit the rocks below
Once tapped,
The ripples
Resonate like thunder
To the heart chamber
Blocking out the oxygen
Bleeding the veins dry
As Arizona dust
Cold as a fallow
Norfolk
Field in winter,
Until the threads
Are brittled and
Littered with lies
Of smiles

Connecting
Nothing with nothing
A
Mere
Appendage to despair

The Penis Prayer

I do not regret my relationship with Jeffrey Epstein. The people that I met and the opportunities that I was given, either by him or because of him, were actually very useful – Andrew Windsor

I shall
Not
Go
Where
I have
Not
Been

Invited.

Dictum Factum

Here is the dull earth to build upon undecorated – Louis
MacNiece, *Twelfth Night*

Do not halt your dreaming
For a verb symbolises action
We have feet still
For walking,
If we open our eyes again
Tell me of your seeing,

The sun, this day
Is rising
Slowly, the earth
Is warming
The light, indiscriminately
Spreading
But still so much work
Needs doing,
As at this time
There are so many
Dying
So be unafraid to show
Your crying,
As grief the price of
Loving
Let our tears fill the fountain
When there are others
Who needs our
Holding
Step lightly with our going
And be steadfast with our staying,
Love, too

Can be
Contaging,
Even when it seems
It is
Fading,
Be grateful for the light of
Morning,
And sink into the darkness of
Evening,
In winter
Become as trees
Accepting
There needs to be a
Shedding,
And in   spring,
Unmanacle your voice
And let the world
Hear your
Singing,
And so,
Allow yesterday to be
Educating,
Tomorrow be filled with
Hoping,
But
Today
Today
Overflow
With
Being,

A Little Patience

You admitted that the
First time you had sex
With him
Was in the changing room
Of the hotel spa
Where you worked
On the night
Of a Gary Barlow
Tribute concert

Doesn't seem the best subject
For a poem
But I have too much time
On my hands right now
Plus it gives me
The chance to research
The collected works
Of the uppity tax dodger
At least

Did you prompt the unholy meeting
With ARE YOU READY NOW?
Did you think
COULD IT BE MAGIC?
Did he put his
ARMS AROUND ME
Did he call you
BABE
Was it
EVERYTHING I WANTED
As you sneaked into the sweaty locker room
As the band played on?

Was it
FACE TO FACE
Was he your GOD
Did he whisper HANG ON IN THERE BABY
Did you
LAY DOWN FOR LOVE (co-written with Richard
Stannard… no me neither)

I guess LOVE WON'T WAIT
Was he MR EVERYTHING
Did he make you SING
Were you on your knees
Yet not to PRAY
Did you feel any
SHAME (co-written with Robbie Williams of course)
I read he did a cover of
EVERYBODY HURTS
I imagine you didn't hear that one
As he ended the set with
LIE TO ME
Did your lover
say
IT ONLY TAKES A MINUTE
And WHY CAN'T I WAKE UP WITH YOU?
Because I'm married you twerp (actually better title)
So it became a
REQUIEM
A cover for
You saying LET ME GO

I waited in the car park to pick you up that rainy night
You asked WILL YOU BE THERE FOR ME
I was, at midnight
Unknowing of what had just unfolded

Quite sad really
I would have enjoyed the show
Especially as I now know
All of his fucking songs

So yes,
EVERYTHING CHANGES
And I SHALL NEVER FORGET
The look on your face
When I said
I didn't want you
BACK FOR GOOD
So yes
I guess
After 15 years of marriage
And 3 of lies,
I really didn't have much
PATIENCE
After all

The Lie

I found the lie again this morning
I shouldn't have looked
but I'm sorry, I did,
searching under beds
and amongst names,
it lay so still, I wasn't sure if it was still alive
so I poked it,
held it, almost cradled it
took it outside
into the bright sunlight
gave it the kiss of life
it grew and grew
stood up once more
stretched and looked at me
then walked away, shouting names,dates,times,clues
and crimes.

I ran after it,
clawing, stumbling through thicket,
tried to stop it going
knocked it to the floor kicked and punched it
till it lay lifeless once more,
I picked it up,
carried it inside,
as before,
I hid it in a secret place
closed the door
swallowed the key
and sat in the sun
I know where the lie is now,
but I can't tell anyone
what I have done.

Fucking Echoes

Sometimes
I think I glimpse you in the hazy light
Of a summer street
Like the ones
We'd see whilst on holiday
After swimming at the beach
And we'd dress in white cottons
And drink cold cokes
In twilit cafes
Where they'd serve bread
With the meal
And the sun
Would set on the edge of the orangeblue horizon
And for a moment
Everything seemed to be whole
As the collared doves
Cooed us into idyllic aftermath of
collaboration
Then stop
I remember
How you were fucking
Someone else
And sending coded messages
As I swam in the crystal sea
To him
Ripples like echoes
And the photos I took
Of you on your phone
Were not for our album
But him
For future fucks and fucks and fucks and fucks and fu

13

Sometimes
I think I glimpse you in the hazy light
Of   a   summer   street
Then stop
And turn around,

and
Let
The
Image
Die   Before   It kills   m   e.

Rementia Song

We are walking around the National Museum of Wales
Visiting Ivor Davies' *Silent Explosion*
Exhibition
Sheep skulls, flooded homes,
Destroyed dialects
Books gashed by guns
A testimony of abrasion

Words wander in
From a remembered past
Commas glisten,
Holding, holding
Their own
For a brittle moment
A shining slice of time
Before
The full stop stamps its mark upon the mind
Voices shake
As stories are shared
The air shimmers with the tears of trembling time

A dew settles upon parchment
Ink blots of foreverness
A Rorschach mapping
Smudged across the vociferations of neverness
Forged into mental monuments
And shakily offered
Like hands reaching out to
Some misted memory

A cracked bowl
Becomes

A metaphor
Our very existence
Grandmothers appear
At the stove
Rivers
Pour pure recollection
Blasted books
Brim with abandonment
If only we
Listened
Listened
To the silent explosions
Of
Love,   loved and   loving,

The Guerilla Tapestry (2021)

That is the secret of happiness and virtue— liking what you've got to do. All conditioning aims at that: making people like their inescapable social destiny. – Aldous Huxley, *Brave New World*

We
Are not deceived by your words
We see through your promises
We sanctify your lies
We
Are the disaffected
The isolated wounds of subtle napalm
Shopping doesn't make us happy
Commercials cull our sensitivity
Freedom is nothing without responsibility

And in these rain drenched tarpaulins of the market traders
Lies the epitome of belief
Clinging to our pennies
An entrance or exit
A memory of a dream
This hole in my throat
This gap in the ink
This place without meaning

This stuttering eloquence of screaming
So save
Save us all
Allow desolation
Find a path
Be unafraid to act
Hold life
Stand stand stand oak tall

Even the smallest body makes a shadow
In the hanging out of washing
This protest of discipline
These tiny hands scraping solitudes
Clinging to moments
Creating miracles from everyday routines
In the dignity of ironing
The anxiety of mortgages
The the the
Sentence of being
But still still still
The being
We are butterflies trapped in the frost
Victory is acknowledging the fact that we
We have not yet lost
So caress me with your alienation
Alienate me with your caress
Create me with your credit
Pour me power through voting for brexit
Feed me freedom from selling shares
Paint me a symbol and tell me i'm free
We are we are
The guerrilla tapestry
The silence of insurance payments
Council tax reductions
Industrial tribunals
The penny pinchers
Super savers
The lottery watchers
We are we are

The incoherent throats searching for sound
The peaceful protestor
The Black Lives Matter marcher
Extinction Rebellion campaigner

Yes cymru speaker
The single mother
The social worker at the homeless shelter
We are
The happy shoppers
Credit cravers
Sales offers
Foodbankers
Poundstretchers
The breaking fabric of modernity
Stitched only by our solitude
We are
The temporary fragments of a capitalist master plan
Unemployment statistics
Family credit beggars
Starving asylum seekers
Nocollarcoolies
Zero hour slaves
Deliveroo drivers
Debt drowners
Sucking severances
Praying for meaning
Not this stuttered screaming
This pathetic attempt at standing
And in these motives that purify
In this act that dignifies
And in this tiny gesture of defiance
Is an articulation of a void
Of a vision versed in lament
This hate this hate
Is born from love
If George Floyd couldn't breathe
Then neither can we
dim cyfiawnder dim heddwch
no justice no peace

We, we are the undying
The breath of chlorophyll over the concrete
We are loneliness burned
Iron fists fuelled by injustice
We are the denied
Yetunified
We are the tapestry
The crackling cracks of modernity
Dislocated desperations stitched together
By the disparate verses of our skin
I write therefore we exist
We exist therefore i write
And from this page this scream
This no
From the hospital to the dole
From the library to the care home
Is the sound of
The alone to   the   alone
The sound the silence the sound the silents
Of the ability to resist
And in this ink the blood of 1000 miners
The hands of uncounted refugees
The tongues of annibyniaeth
The struggle of my father
The sensitivity of my mother
And the future of my children
And in this prison cell there is the skysunlight
And in these words the power they try to deny us
And in this ink
Is one
Is many
Is you and i
And with this voice
Others that raise together
That refuse to surrender

To their demands that pressure
man to mother
She   they   him
Woman to child
This guerrilla tapestry spread nationwide

And in this division
There is a unity
In this incision
There is a sanctity
And upon this pale silent page
Blisters
A cacophony enraged
With the spirit of generations
Following the dream of emancipation

We are we are
The threads
We are we are
The severance
We are we are
The stitches
We are we are
A no in search of a yes
We are we are
The breaking
We are we are
The making
The lost beginning to find
We are and shall be
The guerrilla tapestry
Gobaith Gwybodaeth
Your hand in mine
Gorymdeithio ymlaen,
Ymlaen,

Lunghold

A soft once of your breath
Arrives
Like candlelight
Scoring its shadow
Across my face

Imprint
Imprinted
Loss,
grown
as December crocuses
feel for the sun
that occasions
a drought
when all is done
but would i
could i
offer you my oxygen
once more
a then, now?
As my alveoli inflate
To stem the end
As your names spin off
In the storm
Hurricaning inside
Of my
Yes,
Yes,   yes

Demonise Or Die

for Stephanie Bottrill

*The increase in value of the world of things is directly proportional
to the decrease in the value of the human world*
– The Communist Manifesto

As they sat in their splendour
Planning new modes of attack
They discovered the spare room supplement
Better known as the bedroom tax

A cunning concoction of laissez-faire and big brother
A meticulous maledicta
That sets one against another
And each to judge the other

As starbucks and amazon find new ways to fall beneath the radar
The most vulnerable, the sick, the poor
Are targeted by ids, the moral crusader
Also known as the societal raper

Bedrooms counted
Benefits slashed into the negative
Economic policy parades as moral imperative
Blame spews from a capitalist fundamentalist

In one swoop of his rhetoric,
The euphoric pronouncements whose agenda is desecration

That abhors waste
And values austerity
Admonishes food banks for charity

Yet
Elevates man to man inhumanity
Under the guise of free marketed economy

When nothing goes in
Nothing comes out
Survival the staple
Existing, those labelled
As thought processes starved with doubt
Choice becomes
Blankets instead of heat
Food banks placed in schools
Place the non payers on the ducking stool
Until community
Until care
Until unity
Become obsolete
'You have nothing to fear
It is a proud duty to provide
Financial security
To the most vulnerable members of society
And this will not change' – ian duncan smith, 2010

That was then
This is now
As today i read of those
Threatened with letters
Sent by their betters
Atos interviewers
Benefit reviews
Then
Suicide notes
From freezing cold flats
Pushed to the edge

By duncan smith's pledge
To reduce the stats
As they sit in their shiny safe splendour
Planning the next attack
Taking pride in their new mortuary slabs
Upon which lie
The victims of their
Subtle solution

The bedroom tax

Residual

One gets used to loneliness
The way an old cardigan moulds
To your shoulders
Crumples you in
Its fraying ends an oversized blanket,

Yet it is the one that calls to you
Every morning
Especially in winter
It is hardy
A safety shield on those white breath mornings
When you wish another hand would flick the
Kettle's switch to make
That first cup of steaming tea

One gets used to anything in the
End
You discard the velvet jacket
Throw away the leopard print shirt
And
as
The cardigan becomes the only thing
You wear
Ever,

You look around
One day
And
Realise
That someone else
Has been buttoning it up all this time,

You

for my father

Tell me
How
When as a child
You went to the circus
And took a penknife
Hidden in your pocket
'just in case'
you say.

The tent didn't collapse that day
But the picture always stayed with me
And
As life threw its lances
Its other
Possible smotherings
You were prepared
For the failing light.
Pen knife
By your side
A way out
is a way in
and
you always had those exits marked
then,
on
that silent morning
when I found you in bed,
everything in its place
in our home,
I saw your penknife

On the fridge,
Open,

Sharpened,   Ready,
I pick it up,

Just   in   case,

Mornings Teach Us Shadows

I have started to fold early
Death has killed off a part of my living
A murder of moments
Sucked deep in the stomach
Of bare survival
Clinging to the routine
That fastened us
Together:
The post-match football call
The sudden spiral of a scratched vinyl
The Sainsbury's list
Ah to hold one of those
Phonetic bastard epics
Would lance the boils that poison
My words upon no shoulder
Left to lay upon
Gone all gone gone all gone
Yet
Present in this treacling time
Of invisible torture
Of the song that refuses to sing
So the tongue mimes its days
As shadows teach us mornings,

Trawsblaniad Enaid/ Soul Transplant/ Ruh Zara'Aa

These don't look like children to me – We should do dental testing to certify the age of refugees – David Davies MP
There are no borders in space – Russian Cosmonaut

May the Syrian soil
beneath your fingers
fuse with the Welsh earth
to meld into a new garden

may you take refuge in Tryfan's crags
and wander wild up Pen y Fan
may your bread rise
with the blown beach winds of Ogmore and
Rhossilli

May you bring sunshine to our vineyards
may the Teifi Elan and Taff
bring you home when you are lost

Let the slate mountain of Blaenau Festiniog
build a roof to protect you
from the nightmares of your past
and the deep reservoirs moat
your fears

let the tongues of Bevan Cadwaladr and Glyndwr
be your advocate against
throats of hatred

Let Cymraeg chime with Arabic
to forge our new language
may your children grow like the
rings of the Langernyw Yew
sutured and secured to this land

May you spice our larder with
falafel and fattoush
And let us share food at Arthur's table
and
seek shelter in Carreg Cennen's secret tunnel
and awake as poets
from the slow slumbers of Cadair Idris'
dawn drenched slopes

Let the salted arc
of Cardigan Bay
soothe   the scars of yesterday

and may you stand upon
the aching arches of Pumlunon
to view this tiny massive land
from where
the Severn, Rheidol and Wye birth their journey
and you too, can flow

May the cradling arms of the Cambrians
strengthen you
Yr Wyddfa's mist shawl you
and the valleys cwtch you
as 'na thelyn berseiniol fy ngwlad'
(nor silenced the harp of my country)
Because
it now has a new string

from an end to
a just begun

For
we are all transplanted
from somewhere
brought by the breeze
from sea to shore
settled on fallow ground
grateful for the sunlight
waiting for the rain

And if they try to bury us
we shall dig deep
sprout roots
cling to our past
and from the lived present
invent our future
yours and mine
come,
let us cultivate oak and olive trees
side by side
ochr yn ochr
and
Daw eto haul ar fryn

To Be Or Not

for all the children being denied the chance to study English/Welsh literature at GCSE

you think your pain and your heartbreak are unprecedented in the history of the world, but then you read. – James Baldwin

Not Duffy Shakespeare Taliesin or Angelou
Because you, you see, are in set two
So those words are not for you

For we need to prepare you for the workplace situation
Cvs letters forms and basic comprehension
To make you ready
For zero hour contracts minimum wage
And strict regimentation

No time for Miller Sassoon or Ishiguro
Oh no those words are not for you
Because you boys and girls are in set two

No room for character motivation, metaphor
or Barrett Browning's sonnets
Why so astonished?
Think of this as a mind colonic
Just dot the i's and fill in the gaps
Know your place know your class
You'll be surprised how quickly each lesson passes

As expression only distracts
And we cannot afford any cracks
So learn by rote and memorise the facts
All we are concerned about is how you can make a profit
What is more important, a dream. Or a full wallet?

So it shall be literature for those who will pass it
And language for those who are dull
And in the selection of the brightest
All poetic aspiration is culled

No chance to escape the margins
No colours but the teacher's red pen
Where the sun is merely a noun
And writing's just a means to an end

And what of love?
Of Walcott's mirror
What of doves?
Of Niemöller's horror?

And what of the compass to this land
Of Hedd Wyn's Gogledd
Clarke's West
And Davies' Bells of Rhymney
What of the
Caneuon fy nghwlad?

How to be yourself
Beat bullies, accept others
And
Navigate the world with truth and empathy?

When you are trapped in classrooms outwardly benign
Where the bookshelves
Gather dust not spines
A place of cvs and full stops
And the application forms   await the primark sweatshops

And
And i think of my own dear mother
Reading bedtime stories to me
And all the dead poets' blood
spilled in their eloquent lonely pleas
For
Love imagination and humanity
As Lorca Sexton
Saro Wiwa Plath and Larkin
Now circle in skies so lost
For they have no place to alight on
As all literary dreams lay quashed
Except for those select few at the top

Five
** the clock really is striking thirteen
Four
And the pupils are asleep in what had once been the gymnasium
Three
And april is the cruellest month
Two
That was me. that is alex and my three droogs
We all learnt to love big brother

And
One

I now know why the caged bird sings, sings   sings…
Zero

Because
No Duffy Shakespeare Thomas Angelou or Wilde
For you boys and girls
As you are now in set five
We want you to exist and survive
Not question and thrive
and those words
those worlds
Will never
Be yours
No matter how hard you try.

The Dark Engraving

the ink is drying
blank pages scatter the fields
that we once filled with our birdverbs
now
nouns stand like scarecrows
under winterboned skies

I etch insolent adjectives
into battered notebooks
dust coats bookshelves
the dictionary lost in historical romance
poets bow their heads
priests scatter ashes
your lies drained me tearless
took my tongue away
and stapled it to the electric fence
then tempted thunder
with your atrophic speech
and covert sentence
you whispered to others
never me,
forced me to my knees
to receive cowardly communion
stuffed pages of pretence
into my mouth
as I begged for more
for more more more

your selfish sermon
of blameless infidelity
then
silent ambiguity

of your terms
a glossary of adultery
framed by proxy
as you wrote
clichéd couplets
from a secret diction
designed to placate
and avoid
detection
how
the staccato stanzas
stabbed me senseless
held on to my character
like a riverbank in torrent
we lived ellipsis
by,
omission,
as I became
a master of semantics
armed with heart
and phone records
digging and connecting
I was sentenced
in my absence to an existence
of mimesis
I walked in the brackets of our marriage
as you ignored the semicolons

and
now

how
I stammer and struggle
to

find

the

f
u
l
l

STOP,

Meditations Upon The Mundane

1/ Washing the dishes

can save marriages
halt arguments
settle debates with silence
and
cleanse the debris of a dank day

the soaking away of dirt
the glued porridge bowl
that someone forgot to scrape

as cups and saucers
washed
rinsed with cold water
set to drip-dry efficiently
the way the hot tap
scalds and scours ingrained teenage late-night snack detritus

the methodical ritual of
scrub
then rinse
then place
a dna thrum of routine
passed on from life to life

that fixes our feet
firmly upon the floor
a monument of self discipline
a route to peace
a safety blanket of accomplishment
that cleanses the soul
daily,

2/ Vacuuming in the nude

We shed our selves daily,
Pieces chip off like china cups
Skin sheared days
Where we cannot even step outside the front door

And we wonder where
All the dust comes from?
We walk past
 Pretend to ignore
dance
The dereliction away
But then
One day
We find ourselves
Barricaded in
By
Ourselves
And
Our detritus
So we bring out the vacuum cleaner
And suck it all up
Into the bagless wonder
And tip it out into the bin
Then
Begin to ready ourselves
For the shedding
All over again,

3/ Window cleaning for the soul

For Matilda

On that day
That catches us
Quite unaware
In early march
After endless misted drizzle
When the sky
Blows itself clean
And paints
A blue patina of empty fullness
As the sun fireflies
Upon our tiny empires
And illuminates our negligence
We pull the blinds up
To see the dusty blotches upon the glass
And
We reach for the spray bottle
Of window cleaner
That has laid dormant for months
And that bunch of cut-up old tea towels
We blink
And begin to clean
The window
Like
There
Is
A tomorrow
To be seen,

Reeva Steenkamp and Me

Discretion is the polite word for hypocrisy. – Christine Keeler

They made us out to be the huntress, the whore
Made us wear their disguise
The invisible one
And the photographed one
My body I began not to recognise
Made me hate myself to the deepest core
Despise and be despised
That's how they begin their war
The male gaze corrupted my womanhood
In their need to feminise
So began the lies

And you
They couldn't even remember your name
Girlfriend of
Model
Reality tv star
Partner of athlete
Never Reeva   go on   say it
Men of the privileged life
Reeva,   Reeva Steenkamp
Beautiful intelligent woman, woman
29 years old
When he shot you that screaming night
He
Yes that's right
He   him   it
Partner of Reeva Steenkamp
Boyfriend of Reeva Steenkamp
Murderer of Reeva Steenkamp

Can't remember his name now
But I, we
Will remember yours
Reeva

As everyone remembers Profumo
Doting hubby
Charity worker
CBE
Citizen of The British Empire
And I, a slutty Anglo Marilyn Monroe
Call girl, escort, self serving liar
Smoke and mirrors
Cocks and cum
Where they put you on your knees
Then sweep it away like
It never happened
after they've had their fun

I was incarcerated by their greed
Found guilty by insecurity
They wanted me in bridal gowns
And red leather gags
Instead of tenderness
They choked me with privileged plump hands

It took me 30 years to tell my story
To walk away from that chair
I am more than the woman who Profumo had an affair with
It took you, Reeva, 30 seconds to lose your name
You are more than a murder victim
That some wanted to blame
Christine
Christine and Reeva

And the thousands of other women
Raised on a pedestal then
Crucified by their controlling games
Weinstein Trump Kavannagh   Johnson Windsor
Clifford Pistorius Epstein
To preserve their power
They destroy another's
Lined up like an assembly line
Scapegoats for their failings
Souls as men's playthings

But we shall not die if you say our names
Reeva Steenkamp and Christine Keeler
Human beings not meat   for THEIR USE
Reeva Steenkamp and Christine Keeler
Speak our names and it is US who shall accuse

Extra Time?

The hardest times
Are born from the most beautiful times
three o'clock Saturdays
as the sun would dip and the radiator clunked
and the comforting tones of Jeff Stelling drift in
I knew where you'd be
Listening in
A haze of pipe smoke
And maybe ironing
A safety net of time
Keeping an eye on Leeds Cardiff Swansea Newport and
If the ball filled the net
a gentle telepathy across winter afternoons
and
now
I still watch out for those four teams
A sort of shawl to wrap myself
In your absence
My son
Out with his friends
Texts to tell me Leeds are two up against Cardiff
I go to call you
Last called 31st July 2019
When the grounds rang silent
And the armbands were adorned
Then
Catch myself
Breathe
And remember the final whistle
But
It seems to me
As Cardiff equalise and

the minutes tick
And the numbers rise
That somehow there is an eternity of injury time
Time, time   time
Yeah,
I'll take the bruises

Where The Songs Come From

Until the middle Pleistocene Britain was a peninsula of Europe,
connected by a massive chalk anticline, the Weald-Artois Anticline
across the Straits of Dover

what melodies ripped from ravaged cities
choruses carved from what we lost
a throat has many tributaries
that feed its Oceanic voice
swollen tides bring the detritus of a dream
see how driftwood settles on deserted beaches

Bringing the song in
from silence shall love begin
let difference be our instrument
let the choir begin

from the streets of Aleppo
to the crags of Ben Nevis
within the Norse heartbeat
the cadence calls to us all

in the gentle hands of Victor Jara
to the throats of Alaska
the chants of Native Americans
the rhythm of the African drum

embedded in the elegies of a million deaths
buried in the submerged mud of Doggerland
in the flowing tongues of the Seine, Thames, Rhine, Meuse
and Scheldt
before the Storegga slide
footprints of a borderless age

heartstamps of a unified earth
thunder claps and avalanche crash
raging winds and saltspattered seas
healing wounds with iridescent syllable spill
finding ears with vociferous verse
yes, there was singing
but not as we know it

Bringing the song in
from silence shall love begin
let difference be our instrument
let the choir begin

Gwrandewch/Listen

We are refusing this application because the short term impact of Nitrogen Dioxide (NO2) may cause a detrimental health impact in the locality. The evidence of increasing air pollution and ill health effects is strong and any deterioration of local air quality is likely to have an adverse health and wellbeing impact to a deprived community. – Natural Resources Wales 2017.

Hazrem Hazardous Waste Recycling Plant is built in Cwmfelinfach in 2021. It will emit 20,000 tonnes of Carbon Dioxide into the atmosphere every year.

But in the hearts of those who understood. Forever.
One woman's last stand for St. David's Wood
– Irene Jones

Won't you
take a minute to stop
Turn away from your screen
Put down your credit card
Switch the adverts off
Halt the chain saw
Lower your hunting guns
Turn off your engine
And listen.
Gwrandewch

To the wind
That sows the seeds of tomorrow
Stop Listen.   Notice.

Stop listen notice
To the sunrise's golden gleams through polluted haze

And the forests' trembling roots in our ignorant blaze
The ice floes melting away in silent demise
And the crows' cacophony against poisoned skies
The stoic beach hymning in the plastic swarm
The mountain stretching in the littered dawn
Calling out, to, into, from

This rhapsody of resilience
Is screaming.
Stop.
Listen. Gwrandewch
Notice.
then
Act
Before we end in oblivion

She Threatens To Leave The Union

What? You dare, you just dare,
No one will want you, you know
You're nothing without me. You you can't function without me
Who'll pay the bills, Who will bring home the bacon?
No one will love you ever again –
Look, I'm sorry ok I really am
And I mean it this time I just don't know what comes over me
I, I didn't mean to hold you underwater.
Sorry I put my hand over your mouth.
I know I should have let you speak.
I was only protecting you
From those I thought
Weren't good for you.
It's a blur. Everything goes red.
I thought you were seeing someone else. I panicked.
I thought you were going to leave me for them.
I'm sorry I took your bank card away
And made you wear my clothes.
It made me feel safe. I'm sorry.
It's only because I love you so much.
Look. I'll take you for a meal. Get dressed up.
Wear. Whatever. You want.
I've changed. Promise. Trust me
The extension. I'll get it done. Promise.
This time. Change our life for good. For good. I'm sorry.
I love you.
What?   A divorce.
You dare, you dare. I'm warning you.
Stop, stop or you'll never see the kids again. Ok.
Now just calm down that hot head of yours
And listen to me.
You know it's the right thing to do.

You don't need anyone else.
Annibyniaeth.
Pardon? I told you about that.
So speak fucking English will you?
Wash your mouth out –
Independence?
Ha, you'll need crutches when I've
Finished with you.
Oh shut up. It's just banter.
So, shall we get ready to go out?
I said…   Where, where are you going?
I said,   Where. Are. You. Going.
You dare, you just dare,

Gasliten

1/ An inventory of scars

slowly, somehow,
they get you
Layer by layer
They peel you away
From yourself
Into themselves
A nudge there
A push there
Turning the lights down

So you stumble and reach out
For something to hold onto
And they are there
With salvation hands
Pulling you
Deeper in
stitching
your vulnerability into their insecurity
weaving their wants tighter and tighter
until you are
entangled
into their barbed mire
that masquerades as care
harlequin vultures
gorging on living cadaver
figure skating upon transparent skin
carving their rituals into retina
a sickle cell amnesia
violating the amygdala
forcing adrenalin where serotonin should swim

pumping cortisol for survival
threat detector body protector memory collector
at the indifferent hands of
the savage saviour
the master puppeteer
somehow, slowly
they get you on your knees in the half light
a giddiness in the gloaming
an unction of enmity
inoculated by fear
a poisoned umbilical
direct to the atrophying heart
with
an ellipsis of sepsis
as you begin
to   end
unless,

2/ Vortex

I remember the night
You came home late
After 'visiting Debbie'
You turned off the bedroom light
Undressed
Slipped into sheets

And pushed yourself against me
I clung to your torso
Suckled soft breasts
Yet
Tasted semen
On your nipples,
Choking,
I thought of the sea
The swelling carcass of night
And what it would
Be like to sink
Alone
Under the Atlantic sky
I called to you

But
You had already
Departed,
I carried on swimming
Drowning, drowning deep in you

3/ Armamentarium

Until the day
When I glimpsed that diaphanous sunrise
That meticulous morning
When I finally silenced the march of that maledicta
As I bathed in the fleeting flurry of the flame
It illuminated the dust that had accumulated
I shook open the curtains
The chains clattered upon the cold tiles
I hadn't seen the bookcase for years

How could this be life?

Feasting on toxicity
Doubting my own fragile reality
As my memory cowered in your darkening light
I rose, like that sun
That daystar shedding its incandescent photons
I rose,
In pieces
Yet with peace
And began to navigate my own destiny again
Reclaim the broken narrative
Walk on that lie eroded path
And faced myself in the mirror
And saw that I had become the light
The light, the   light

4/ Daylight of the fading

sometimes,
the only way to hold on
is to let go,
slowly, somehow

Fossilise

There is grandeur in this view of life, with its several powers,
having been originally breathed into a few forms or into one; and
that, whilst this planet has gone cycling on according to the fixed
law of gravity, from so simple a beginning endless forms most
beautiful and most wonderful have been, and are being evolved. –
Charles Darwin, *The Origin of Species,*

No one could learn the song except the 144,000 who had been
redeemed from earth – these are those who did not defile themselves
with women for they keep themselves pure – Revelation 14

an inbred arrogance
threads through time
into arteries and brainstem cortex
passed on like defunct dna

to wither thought
capture moments in amber
and strengthen reason
into belief
as the child digs in the soil, she finds
remnants of another day
a far off starlit day
whole worlds trapped in
collapsed mud and clay,
crushed breaths
tourniquetted in time
a pompeii in miniature
lives frozen for us,
to imagine and escape into
for a day,

statues standing still
in sheltered soil
dormant dancers move again,
shattered bones hold the pain
as innocent eyes catch glimmers of a then,
that helps us to
understand the now
with, with
the if
as
flint fed forgetting cloaks the churches
and sandstoned serenade evades the synagogues
as the mulchmoorland peat
is held off limits by mosque tannoy
and imam indifference

fossilised mannequins
preaching death
forever rocks
ciphering codes to kids
flies in amber
mouthing words
that strangle tongues
stone surveyors of an ancient living landscape
that avoids their petrified gaze
as the child's hands dig into history,
illuminate mystery
with a hammer and chisel
and searing vision
to make that historical incision
freed from the sectarian straitjacket of religion
their exploration
our future
their knowledge

our past
their malleable minds
rising through rock and stone
their digging
our windows
their evidence
our wonder
their riverminds
flowing through time
their clarity
misting our eyes,
into into,
revelation;

A Contagion Of Courage

April 2nd 2020 – NHS frontline staff Amged El-Hawrani, Adil El Tayar, Habib Zaidi, Thomas Harvey, Alfa Saadu, Areema Nasreen and Aimee O' Rourke have died saving others' lives during the Coronavirus pandemic in the UK.

As Charles Windsor, Balmoral
Jumps the queue for a Covid 19 test
The staff at Prince Charles Hospital (NHS)
Merthyr Tudful
Face each day, to work, to care
At the point of need, with little rest
anxious, worried, under duress

Is it fair, can it be moral
Can't there be a commitment
That those saving lives
should not lose theirs
Because of lack of Personal Protective Equipment
Who will take the blame
for this willful negligence
those in power
should hang their heads in shame
judging doctors nurses carers to be disposable, irrelevant

For where the marketplace and the public school unite
When, just like a war, an indifferent monolith
Sends us off to fight
Unarmed fodder to face the bombs
Where less and less come home
A frontline apocalypse
In the name of power politics

And as Cummings leaves number 10
Scuttling to self isolation
And Andrew hides in his taxpayer paid mansion
The care workers go into houses
And nursing homes
Timed, zero houred
Unprotected
To bathe to dress those who cannot, with selfless compassion
Risking sickness and infection

They clapped the NHS last week
Yet for decades they've been trying to dismantle it
To amputate its reach
To starve its core
Quid pro quo,
Telling us it is not fit for purpose anymore
Wasn't everything on the table not so long ago?

And now I don't think BUPA or Spire are saving the dying
I only see The National Health Service
Upon which people are relying
To help and care and soothe and save
72 years on from '48
Still trying to eradicate
Want Disease Idleness Ignorance and Squalor
So maybe it is time
To not just clap but
To honour,
Those who face the daily horror
and risk their lives
So that we can recover and survive

And let us catch
Their contagion of courage

And echo
Their roar of resilience
A living vaccine to this deathly virus
Let it educate and nourish
Maybe it will deliver us
From the money laundered neo liberal idiots
Who believe health is a business
Yes
A   National   Health   Service
Say it strong shout it loud
The clue is in the name
It is a verb as well as a noun
And
It.   Is .   Not .   For.   Purchase.

As of April 2021 nearly 250 NHS staff have died due to Coronavirus

Notes Towards Forgiveness

I have carried fire
For aeons
Threaded through veins
Tied onto tongue
And sung by lungs
My mouth is parched
By my scorched earth policy

What can grow anymore?
I am becoming dust
Burning embers/ Numb nerves/ Shredded empathy
Scratching throat
Desperate for water
To dampen the flames
I have begun to melt
Like lead
I am dribbling
Trying to find the sand
I have lsot my hsape
I splatter/ clatter/ scrunch and hunch
In the flooding of feeling
I have forgotten the healing of
Forgiving
By cauterising the wound
I have fossilised the pain
Branded it into my brain
Exist in chains
That started as carrier
Dammed the stream
Till the ocean's out of reach,
All the while
Roasting myself

Praying to the bitter effigy
Of revenge
Soaking in petrol
A soul immolation
In the quest for dissolution
Of us
When
I should have
Allowed air to heal the cuts
And
Let forgiveness
Rejuvenate
Life's fragile pulse;

Dysunitednation (2021)

For Babi Badalov

Everyone has the right to seek and to enjoy in other countries asylum from persecution.
– Article 14: Universal Declaration of Human Rights

in great great britain
land of hope and glory
land of the fucking royal fairy tale story
patrol your borders obey their orders
but we spend £15 million on one trident alone
but close our hospitals and moan
at asylum seekers taking our money
our homes our jobs our liberty
lets lock 'em up before they destroy our economy
'ssssseeeeeeeeeeee
we're lovelee people we ain't no racists
but if they cum yer you'll get ower fists'
in great great britain
this dysunited nation of red. white. and. blue.
of bigotry and children learning through
sun headlines and telegraphed lies
rees mogg proclaims farage denies
as refugees die in front of our eyes
as girls are stoned for falling in love
and men castrated for the forbidden touch
patrol your borders obey their orders
but we welcomed hitachi aiwa toshiba fucking lg
we worship giroud aguero and divock origi
yet we spit at frightened refugees
i propose that next time a politician, neil hamilton or anybody
mentions

the words detention and refugee
so casually –
i will ask them to look in my bible –
the dictionary
where they will see that refuge is the word before refugee
and detente comes before detention
and asylum means place   of   protection
so –

ignore their orders destroy all borders;

ignore their orders destroy all borders;

Ord Fest

We feed each other words
The way
Eagles drop mice to their babies
Clawing and gnawing
Each other's flesh
Voracious vociferations
Spiralling soliloquys
Sensual sonnets
That honey throats
And slide
Down
Thirsty gullets

Whole days
Distilled into
One line
I pour syllabled nectar
Into your
Verbhungry mouth
To sustain our
Love
We
Deify dictionaries
And
Suck thesauruses dry
Savouring
Their inky elegance
And succulent soulfruit
Building freeing sentences
With aching breath
I bite melodies from your lips
Curl your vowels upon my searching tongue

Stroke your hot book spine
Taste moist consonants
Dripping and slipping
Welding and melding
Swallowing you whole

Nutritious
Yet with every drop

I crave for more,

The Memory Parade

Tell me what mattered
Explain to me who was there
Draw me a window
Show me why everyone was so scared

What did people become like
When the crisis hit
Monsters or missionaries
Who was it you stood with?

The givers or the takers
The truth seekers or the fakers
The lonely ones or the baying crowd
What held together as humanity drowned?

In the days of the silence most deafening
Did your voice find itself somehow strengthening?
And.
Humankind –
Can you answer me one question
What was it you left behind?

So that after the darkness disappeared
Someone desperately searching far and near
May find
a clue, a souvenir

That will remind them
How, upon a once time,
Love lived here,

                    Love   lived

Bring It Back Home

If you are irritated by every rub how will you ever be polished?
– Rumi

where there is bile
return to lullaby

when there are fists
hold fast to flowers

when they throw you chains
knit a shawl

if it rains tongues of nails
become a hammer

When they staple our mouths
strum guitars

when they ask for selfishness
stand in solidarity

when they scream for death
scatter sunflower seeds

if they bring starvation
make a soup from your memories

As they sell you perfection
make a crack

When they build walls
design doors

when they preach paradise
close the door
it is here, inside

as they bellow me me me
whisper goldenly
we   we   we

FROM

The Guerilla Tapestry
(1995)

This Terrible Honesty

i don't think i'll ever understand this
these   the
long hours of sorrow stabbed friendship i feel here
so close your eyes/ fold your hands/ lie calm
let this darkness shroud you
let this nightness safe you
this terrible sight of being pierces me with its acid iris of reality;
forcefed on adverts i didn't think people suffered anymore
But
now i know.
for i have seen hands clutch invisible gods at the blue of night
and
i have seen breath scatter sadness
across once childrenned rooms;
i have seen death living
and living dying
in the parchmented lungs spitting out time
of flesh pinned to the bed by morphinned laces
allowing no escape from my sight
i have seen days shed silence into weeks / souls rise to
ceilings/voices fade to mute and i   i   i
am at a loss to explain.
if i were to paint cancer i would splash red and black resin upon a
white canvas and let it drip and clash like oceans of oil –
if i were to act cancer i would curl into a ball and close my eyes
if i were to sing cancer i would scream until i tore my throat to a
million scagged shreds of severance –
if i were to describe this terrible honesty i would ask you to look
into her eyes
they tell no lies they only tell;
But within the candle is the wick and
within/without

77

above/below
the cancer there lays the spirit
a spirit of suffering
a spirit sublime
this colossal caught sunflower speared by sun   yet
diminished by time
a spirit of dignity denouncing a spirit of humility hanging
this inside of pain this outside of smile
spirit how are you so strong in this unbearable bearing this
this
this
eternal trial?
and
beneath hymned eyes brittle elbows and cancercracked skin
i have seen death
But   i
            i have seen life
of a serene soul/ a dying body wept by our load
but the spirit is lying in the calm breeze of a childhoodhidden
road through the grass
glancing a meaning
a meaning at last
of a lucidity from reality a poem a life
this
terrible honesty and i know
that
the brightest star is the deepest scar
the brightest star is the deepest scar

the deepest scar
is our brightest
b   r   i   g   h   t   e   s   t

star.

Philosophy (Father)

for my father

live small. think skies. hold others. deny yourself the luxury of
passivity. find contentment in asking questions. there are no
answers. no. no absolutes. understand that coming is but a
prelude to going. that then and if will always have a now. there.
there is no point in affluence. just another drug. affluence buys
you back. so. so continuously strive for meaningful poverty. the
comfort of children's pictures. of autumn dawn. letterbox.
acknowledge the inked beauty born from struggle. alienation.
aloneness. despair. of tourniquets wrapped so tight your veins
recite epitaphs. epitaphs.
this hand upon hand. this letter upon letter. wound within
wound. this wish within why. this poem next to paint. this
love,
this love stuttering to hate.
of
empathy.
rugged steel symphony. and this pen frightened of saying.
wisdom is not bought at marksandspencers. smallness is the
epitome of success. know the voice inside. watch the birds
upon
rain telegraph wires. the failing. the failing
candle. still. still. casts.
casts a shadow.
of angel.
ink.
solace.
whip.
work.
bled bleeding hands
of stone over soul and fuel within flesh.

so. lip another spectrum. another. another vocal chord.
the
eloquence of
silence.
reaching.   torn.   into.
of sadness. and as time   heaves its burden.
just
like
the stars

we are   free

In The Shadow Of The Birds

i walk
unworthy of their wings
as words whip innocence
sin layers love
sunlight lightens loneliness
shadows
shelter incoherence
mornings   mornings of anxiety
alienation   of   atrophic   modernity
delicate bones
crackling humanity
pavements worn by
faltering fuelling footsteps
generation after generation
hate after hate
tremble after tremble
beauty to the abattoir
lips to the cosmetic
i walk
resembling
iodine
worshipping motrin
frightened of feeling
from this ritalinned meaning
of a throat silence stitched though seeing
a cacophony of simplicity
voice of poppies
memory of metal
a million hours spent watching the skies
and still
i cannot remember what colour it is;
in the shadow of the birds

we are nothing
blanked out references
useless noise   aimless aims
we   will   never   fly
greed nails us to the ground
materials mould rituals restrict
insensation our altar;
the ties of lies
forever impaled upon the corpse of gravity
brain braindeadened –
in the shadow of the birds   i   walk

The First Night On Earth

for Ethan, Evan and Elian

and from this night filled emptiness
comes the harp of day
and out out out to this world
a tiny spark of light
a purity unfurled
this simplicity bringing light
here
begins a stream
unfolds a petal
altering reality to a dream
a rainbow out of the oilslick
a dolphin against the nets
all the tension anxiety and hate i am soon to forget
as he slips and curls

cries   and

clings
as his breath blows away all money and diamond rings.
oh life a clean heart is beating here tonight
oh life a remembrance is forging the future.
out of all the wounds of this modernity
there here everywhere
there flames a bloodbirth of beauty and innocence
amidst the chaos
within this nothingness

begins

Begins
an everything
beginneth here our daily bread

oh make us not dead
beginneth here the poor and the giving
faith and healing
forever and ever
the first night on earth
in
this
moment
i remember
all the other nights
all the other babies that shone into this world in such
nightsunlight
and i think of all their days spent crying
spent
waiting/watching
for signs in the sky and the shadows of guns
i think of them
i think of them
all the dereliction and despair
all the bombed out faces in bosnia
all the fearfilled street children in guatemala
all the homeless across neoned cities
all the gas charred victims of hitler
all the starved eyes of africa
All the Loneliness Aching and Injustice
all of this world
captured in a needlepoint of light
channelled to stick into my veins
and inject me with awareness
as my baby cries
nothing moves
(Everything Feels Forever)
under the grey glaring skies
a lip caught in frost

a tear   a care   a plea
for all that this world has lost
a baby cries
the whole world cries
the constant language of humanity
this image
this now
this everlasting clock tick

i cannot forget/i fumble for threads of connection
and
embark upon humanhood
overflowing with love yet disgusted by life
Here begins Existence
a baby's cry probes my apathy
i rise like steam
i feel like roses
a baby's cry
i remember why
i am a birth
a human
a Nothing
a baby cries on the first night on earth.
i think i understand now
across the world into our Hearts
throughout the Night
glittering us Light
the Father's hands are holding
the Mother's milk is pouring

pouring

pouring
from the past
imagining a future
Darkness is where the Stars are

85

as tonight a baby cries
thinkinghoping
that this night will mould the rest
remembering all the other babies that were ever born
immaculate in their moment.

Loss is where i get my Spine
so find some Meaning Here
hear –

the Father's hands are holding
the Mother's milk is pouring
let the whole world drink
Tonight
we are
Human

oh spirit

Let There Be Days Worthy of this Night

this night.

FROM

The Protest Of Discipline
(1996)

Hiraeth

land of my father what have we done to you
as i look upon these valleyed streets
these stained silent streets of satellite suns that salaciously stare
as i walk these epiphanies of denigration and despair
to live in wales
is to be forever aware
of death –
it is here   there
everywhere   but nowhere
as i stare
at the liposuctioned values and created needs
as chapels close
and spars boom on sunday rained nights of nothingness
as i stare
at these corpse ridden streets of carpet warehouses
poundstretched days lottery dreams and woolworthed wants
we wear our work like leprosy
toshiba   touching toes
aiwa   trapping minds
lg   lacerating dignity
call centres   collapsing community –
factory fucked days spent under the clock of dreaming
grateful just to have a job
in production line economics   money made automatics
so we
struggle to survive
survive to struggle
freedom a credit card spree
is work, are our lives ever free?
so we
buy more feel less
feel less we buy more

we are
atrophy decorated with junk
hands holding a currency of illusion
mouths moving a mind incision
i am nothing
and no thing is
land of my children
what can we do for you?

The Eloquence In The Screaming

still
I know no
thing
all i retain all i articulate is the screaming
the frantic wrenching screaming
from the faces from the throats from the cathode from the
pain from this hate into this love;
but within the catheter borders of the screaming
lays a dripping dying crying eloquence
a terrible vociferation of every soul
we enclose within ourselves;
i retain
i feel a searing eloquence within
of words bathed in barbed wire
echoing in windowless rooms
pages in a grandfather's deathdrawer
leaves in a tornado vacuum,
these are the screams within
these these are the life streams bleeding from skin
for without the screaming there is
no
thing;
and if only you could know what i know
and if only i could know what you know
we could replace the without within
there is no eloquence without the screaming.

this mask i wear pours draughts down my throat
as delinquent thoughts are culled before they can breath
in this reasoned rationed technocracy

an otherness imposed upon from outsideness

inside
i am a bayonet
a volcanic ulcer of expulsion
yet i go nowhere
layered by fear
tarnished by tears
lays the stuttering voice of denial
the silenced dream of action
veining my mind like cocaine
lonely as a hurricane
blinding my eyes with hatred
of myself for i am not;
inside
the placid flesh
a needle ripping for release
feeling for the yellow core of dying beauty within;

silence –

bares the cursed child of freedom
the eloquence in the screaming
through pale corridors of routine
rituals wither sunflower sun
bending like old men at the crack of whip work
we shallow we collapse we consume
to soothe the dereliction
we sit,
we sit like ferns in stone
waiting to sleep –

pouring whitewash into our mouths
the delectable drenching of our souls
by the veneer of illusion
strangling the seed before the sun

can caress the latent power of this lip creation
breathing in alienation
across this factory floored nation
into our minds for more
the white disease –

for more

the belt the greed the maggot the money magic seed
of destruction and defraction
into us it comes
replacing our sad eloquence with the obscene apathy of
'have a nice day it could be you forget it all in an instant he was
killed by friendly fire of collateral damage
and business relations'
smothering the screaming with the businessed smile
the teacher's pen
and the credit sale
seeping into the victims of the lobotomised caress
the destruction of the screaming
to make the place seem cleaner
is the grin of the corporater
the pen of the advertiser
the click of the banker

BUT

between the billboard masturbation
across highways of metallic isolation
there
there lives the deafening screaming of you me us
wiping out the diseased pages of apathy
that bleed our eloquence
with words of amnesia

that forgets the feeling
that chokes our resistance
and
here
there rises the blood of the trees
the blue of the dolphins
the spine of the mountains
the tongues of the tied
arise
arise
a hate eloquence and destroy the death dreaming
and
out there
in there
somewhere
is where
here
there
i desire to speak;
somewhere without limits and fences
sometime without tenses

i
desire
to speak

FROM

Mute Communion
(1997)

Reach

and nothing is perfection
holes
fill
everything
hands fasten in mind distance;
aloneness the companion we cling to
when flesh fails.
if only
only if
repeat
recite
dissonance
of a world unfit for this living.
how
do we signify
what makes contact mean
if and wish constantly recoil into how;
and i cannot find the place for it
it will not enter the space for it.
the
violation
of the one
is the isolation of the two
yet the clock stutters sadness
and time oceans along
indifferent to the apostate of hearts
that once bled together
now stab each other
so
nail hope to the bandage
crush fracture into flowers

can.
can
belonging
ever
belong

again?

11:11:11

listen,
two minutes silence in a century of screams
the rain pours
the poppy will not flower
the flesh bleeds
upon memory
no peace in flanders fields
no rest for saro-wiwa
just the sound of history's necrophilia
and metal detectors scraping sacred soil

you are steel
you are bullet
you are blood
you are broken
and i,
i am a remembrance forgotten
on an antiseptic morning in london
i am a cenotaph souvenir stall selling
you are not

listen,
listen and you will hear
two minutes silence in a century of screams –
no heartbeat to confirm existence
only the bled arteries upon Time
only the white flag deathdrugged and mindunmanmade
from santiago to chechnya
from bethlehem to bosnia
from the somme to the falls road
a bloodfeast of death symphony
a mindfast of sympathy

and as we bow our heads in prayer
listen,
listen
and you will hear
two minutes silence in this century of screams.

Christmas Lights In January

rain beat my soul
empty me in
drizzling distances heart sedated
isolations
isolate
and dignify
as

tears
come to signify
a defiance, a shroud, a loss
a cemetery silence
of uninterrupted eloquence.

strung out like eyes
cold as worship
bleeding blood over sun denied streets
they
watch
they
wait
like Jesus upon Calvary

to be dragged down and put away

until
until

another sense
of
belonging

occurs.

Memoria

there is springtime in death
the wind punished grass cannot be halted
as even in choking there is breath;
the flowers that bloom
are the flowers of pain
in sadness/ in hate/ in defiance/ in despair/
they stab the soil in silence with their fluorescent hymns
they, they shall remain
across parched deserts and money stained streets
in tranquillized bedrooms of illnesslessened bodies
through cracks in the ink
the ravaged rainbow bleeds through.

against the bloodstained canvas of humanity
the petals/ the leaves/ the bulbs/
the mind paints its colour / its renewal
into our lives
though there is a cross
trees still shelter
though bullets replace nails
crucifixion still occurs

there shall be doves
there shall be doves;

in this
blood within wound/ flesh over nails/ sky above man/ weep
into
why
placenta through death
in memory/ in hope/ in hurt/ in plea/
there are seeds planted daily

even though then is pain
today today
shall unfold again
there is springtime in death
there is peace in sorrow
though yesterday burns today
today shall have a tomorrow

Their Life On Their Heads

In a crowd of over 10,000 refugees sprawled across Tuzla's
cornfields, a young woman hanged herself yesterday. No one knew
her name. No one wept for her when her body was cut down from
a tree, and only a single bored policeman kept vigil over the corpse
as it lay abandoned by the gate of the heaving, sweating camp
– The Guardian, July 15th 1995

and we watch
and we watch in our safe homes through marks and spencered
curtains
at the unfolding of another   another celluloid
tragedy
upon insensate sofas feeling sorry for ourselves that we can't
quite
afford that new house or envious of next door's carpet
peering through tunnel visionned lenses at the tv screen;
responding   robotic   rituals
of;
'how terrible-how sad-aren't we lucky-what time is *home and*
away on?'
until it's time to sleep   until it's time to sleep –
we observe, painless puritans pretending to care
we watch   we switch off
we watch   we switch off
then we fall back to our usual apathy and comforted routines
and
lives
as
humanity self immolates like sandcastles upon a beach
the water drowns while we sip evian and remove our facial mask;
through the cathode feed we suck celluloid
stare   stare   at the tv   tvpeople

as millions starve
only needing the basics   we blatantly avoid
in our pathetic attempt to exist while they walk aeons
on incarcerated feet across deserted deserts and desperate streets
only freedom and peace they ultimately seek;
and under this westernised sun
the glare of ozonelessened yellow
that stains their skin   that chokes their throats as flies
settle on week old babies
no mother no father to cling   to no other
but this milk drought of breasts bleeding from this world's sin
and we watch
and i wish someone would cover my eyes
i wish someone would make us see
their life on their heads
a bundle of the past
a complete incompleteness
a future fading fast
their life on their heads
a diet of nothingness
a few grains of rice
a handful of water
dripping dragged from each other's tear bledbleeding eyes
while we we we
choose plastic surgery to remove our third chin
they, the tv people, walk like cancer shedding their skin
and so we watch the tv
voiceless voyeurs inactive activities
we munch our plastic then liposuck the fat

and we watch   we switch off

105

we watch
this unreal reality watchingeatingsleepingwatching
untouchable people weeping impotence into our living rooms

tv   people   what is real?

tv   people   feel the scream   scag my throat
tv   people   cannot touch

tv   people

them   or   us

themorus?

Scalpelandheart

your five fingers growing
beneath this star stemmed sky   and
into the mindlight of anxieties
the moon whispers its words across our silence
entering an everything with verbs of nothing

your five fingers growing
against a crow sky
into this barcoded daylight
that drowns our questions
your five fingers growing
flesh filling flesh
fragile bones bearing witness
sucking/ holding/ clutching rainbows
my hands are emptiness when compared to this

so how can i tell you
that fingers pull a trigger
that hands make a fist   smash jaws
push buttons
hold knives to extinguish a belief in this life/living/live?
how can i hold you with such adulterated palms
and lipsilenced values
when man culls man
for religion   for love   for nothing –

your five fingers growing
attuned to gentleness   cloud   and star
pink miniatures of man
with without this blood bleeding;
and i stare, i stare at your fragile fingers that fuse
how they reach and hold

how they search and ask
how they balance   in air   in sleep
harming nothing
hurting no one
only knowing
the breeze and the breath of brothers and sisters
your touch of harmlessened fingers of fractured foreverness
and so   as night smoothes your eyelids and
sleep slips into skin
i hold your hand   and count my   fingers

FROM

Fuse
(2001)

Of Temazepam And Petroleum

in;
the sky's reflection
splinters into vodka puddles
a lippedpetrol smear upon adolescent   tarmac –

upon;
these tortured sidewalks and hilfigered limbs
a litter of language spilled from lagered tongues

fuckyoucoolasfuckmunwankerwhosaengoanen go on –

so you blank it out you burn it out

of;
acetylene hum of testosterone and
alcopopped   eyes
scanningsulphur   streets
staring   staring   staring

laptopsoftopturboburstcheckshirtoutside
– i wear my umbro jacket though i've never kicked a ball in
mylife –

CAR TRAP BEHIND SHUTTERS
a MECCA of aluminium cadence of stopped docks
IT COULD BE you IT COULD BE you
of jungle beats   mind halts
and acid drops

111

dripping
dripping
from a starwished   sky
of an ironlunged corridor of   whylesswant
and trade
fed by disease and decadence
dancing dancing dancing
in;

the sky's reflection

And What Are You Wales?

an
other
statistic
an
other petalled sympathy another joyrider another drug victim
another factoria another soul
rising rising rising
to the stars above.
we.
we are the fallen the un the dis the in the lost people
we commune with the ghosts of forever upon chapelled
breaths.acned faces pushed tight against mortuary glass staring
staring at the sun –
my son my son.
prozac ain't no bandage to this much blood.
bleeding.bled.it could be you doesn't necessarily mean winning
the lottery
we.
we are holy.we are epiphany.we are full of holes.
holes.holes.holes.
adverted smiles.daz whiteness.hollywood dreams and and and
rhymneyed nights.   silence.
sil   ent stone mountains
greygreat skies staring.staring.
of migrained malls dead work:ingmen's halls.
holding.holding.holding
our lottery numbers like genitals
bowing to zeroes on golden pedestals.
so.design your life.stammer your soul.live the green.plead for
blood.
hold.

heal.

faith.

feeling.

fury

   feel.
an
other.   another.

Demonstrations For Existence

a. the unification

I won't call it a strike. I would call it a demonstration for existence the miners in South Wales are saying, "we are not accepting the dereliction of our mining valleys, we are not allowing our children to go immediately from school into the dole queue. It is time we fought." – Emlyn Williams, 1981

tomorrow

filed away into the redtaped self assurance of office regulations
newlaboured toried amnesia
of the gutwrenched days of dust and blackened blood –

this be the verse of commemoration

of
swallowing servility
spitting out dignity
moulding miracles from whipping work in the belief of a better
place
through education
from a coalclogged face
for emancipation
of a solaced smile
from walking underground miles
of creating a life to be
of communal obligation
of paying for the books in the library

this be the verse of commemoration

through the lies of this fucking century
first
thatchered denial of our fragiled history
now
blair
sits in socialist splendour
ignoring this struggling community
YOU
can call it politics blind us with statistics
starve us with your economics
lie to us with your campaign rhetoric
loud hail about your humanity
BUT
now   now   now

today

as the breathing blisters and lungs cough black
you imprison us with the degrading foreign factory
preach to us about common decency
but as
the eyes and hands that wait for the post to drop
but what about fucking morality
£6000 for a life underground?
your silence is like bedwellty cemetery
but without the stuttered dignity
without the sense of urgency
of 80,000 souls waiting to be heard

this –   this has to stop

and   as

tomorrow

breathes through the green haze of an oxygen mask
let us remember the mountained fresh

yesterdays

of labour, family, dignity and meaning
and let us,   through
these voices
these truths
these histories
these eyes
these lungs
in unity in hope in disgust
exhale
and
let them hear HERE our screaming
let decency prevail
and allow

today   today   today

to be to be TO BE

still breathing

still   breathing –

tomorrow
to   tomorrow

b. selling smiles

what one must seek is integrity and vitality. His holy grail is the
living truth, knowing that being alive the truth must change
— Aneurin Bevan

smile
serve
smile
see
earn
burn
be
smile
serve
see
save save save
grave grave grave
but
made made made
in
wales.
wales.wales.
as fragments of inhumanity
invade our speech invite william hague
to dig a plot
come to wales and get a job
m4 corridor you're not out of reach
so sell me a smile and tie me to the line
make me piss my pants
but get an nvq in making tea
aiwa toshiba hitachi
pyrrhic factories
surrogate mines

a stuttered sense of liberty

so

cellulite my valley

silicone the economy

cross breed fertility

leave behind mind sterility

so

sell me a smile

come to wales and save and smile and serve

and

be

and

see

stare

at

the

sun

and

squint

your

eyes

smile

and

serve

freedom equality and emancipation

no obligation

indelible abrasion

is welsh

for profit –

Nothingland

ONCE WE WERE NOW WE ARE
toll on our personal lives shall i call an ambulance claimline 0800
can you?
SALES OFFERS DOT COM TAKEOVERS
do something hurts in accidents doctor doctor too fast slow
down slow downcan you?
BORDER PATROLLED SOULS
choice is bigger when catch foot and mouth for years and years
UNLIMITED LIMITS
the roses can take care of themselves from kitchen and
bathrooms we
AK-47 CREDIT CARD EPIPHANY
got no brain to carry everything on your back you gotta
WE WALK THE WORLD ON THE INTERNET/SWALLOW
WHOLE
just try   can you?
DAYTIME TV
FUCK BABIES THEN PRAY FOR FORGIVENESS ON
JERRY
SEE IT ALL HAVE IT ALL FORGET IT ALL
FOR AN INSTANT
CHOOSE YOUR AMPUTATION
PAY FOR YOUR DEGRADATION
A SICKLE CELL EDUCATION
good good vibrations looktotomorrow the real ira have claimed
REFUGEE/CATTLE TRUCK/FREEDOM/WORM
INFESTATION
SELF REVERED/RELIGION OF/THE NEW
EMANCIPATION
FOOT AND MOUTH OUTBREAKS
AND GUERILLA ATTACKS
IODINE DENIED

UNDERSTANDING FEIGNED
OR CRUCIFIED
YOU AND ME ME AND YOU US AND THEM WE AND I
WILL NEVER SEE EYE TO EYE
SO WE PLUCK THEM OUT
A SILENT APOCALYPSE
FROM FEARFILLED LIPS

WE SEE NOTHING
WE HEAR NOTHING
WE FEEL NOTHING
WHILE EVERYTHING CRIES AND EVERYTHING DIES
SO GIVE ME MY TAX RELIEF ON MY DEAD OF
COVENANT CHARITY DONATION
BOW DOWN, KNIGHT ME, SHOW SOME
APPRECIATION
A PARAMEDIC POLEMIC
A NARCISSISTIC EPIDEMIC OF DISCIVILISATION
IN NOTHINGLAND/EVERYTHING BREAKS
IN NOTHINGLAND/EVERYBODY TAKES
now news of profit growth and
A SPLENDOUR OF SELF BANDAGES THE MANY
A METHADONE ASSEMBLY SEARCHING FOR
SANCTITY
A GLOBAL CATASTROPHE BEGINS AT HOME
the disease is not present but new supplies are making it to the
shops minister would you please answer the question
IT'S MORE THAN THE SHEEP WE'VE CLONED
CHOKE SLAM MY MIND
CARVE YOUR CRACK UPON MY NECK
IN THIS SELFOCRACY OF THE BLIND
the mortgages of
IN NOTHINGLAND   EVERYTHING GOES
prize money available
THIS FETISH OF FORGETFULNESS

A MESS OF FLESH
THIS PROZAC WILDERNESS
THIS VIAGRAED SPACE SPARKLING
THIS NECROPHILIAC KISS
THAT STINGS
THIS COPROPHILIA OF THE SOUL THAT CLINGS
IN NOTHINGLAND   NOTHING GROWS
one person was deemed responsible
AND SO WE WALK
AND SO WE WALK
standard fares only at this time of day
A HISTORIED LACERATION
it's a high quality finish and will not be beaten on choice or price
with the wider rim it appears more versatile
OF VIRTUAL ISOLATION
THE INSTANT GRATIFICATION A KIND OF
ANAESTHESIA
TO BLANK OUT THE GREYING OPPRESSION
SO FACE LIFT THE PAIN
EYES STILL THE SAME
the benefits of air you'll get that tingling sensation
IN NOTHINGLAND
THE DROWNING DAYS DARKEN
or your money back phone now on
DRAGGING FEET UPON SUICIDE BEACH
RAGGED CLOTHES ON PETRIFIED BACKS
INSIDE THE APPLE MAGGOTS CRAWL
WITHIN THE SOUL WORMS SWARM
more successful more productive
PESTILENT AIR OF INVISIBLE WAR
THE SCARS WE ARE
THE DANCE/ THE DELIRIUM/ THE DYING
THE MUCK OF MAMMON MARKING
THE FIST OF FUCKING HITTING
THESE ARE THE DROWNING DAYS

LIVING SMALL IN MANNEQUIN LAND
COMPANY CRASH FINANCIAL NEED
I'VE LISTENED TO AUTOMATED HELPLINES
UNTIL MY EARS BLEED
£5 for one £12 for 2
you can
you can
I'VE STAYED SILENT FAR TOO LONG
THIS MOUTH TOO STARVED TO FEED
I'VE SEEN THE MOUNTAINS CRUMBLE
I'VE SEEN THE CHILDREN STOOP
BLEACH ONLY CRAVES THE DIRT LIKE THE NECK,
ROPE
a puff of smoke a blade of grass here today gone tomorrow
LIPOSUCTION CAN ONLY REMOVE WHAT WAS
NEVER
THERE
LIKE
NOTHINGLAND
thy will be done
you can you can
I WHICH I NEVER WAS
thy will be done
john 21 verse 2
you can   you can   YOU CAN   you can
ONCE WE WERE
the beauty of submission
the beauty of su—

NOW WE ARE
                        WE ARE.

all lower cases lines taken from cable tv channels

Heartwork

but
behind ache
we place
garden in sleep to recall
one moment under music we sing/
dream/
truly
of   on   to
love
falling go going gone go
but

whispering

wanted   still   always

a diamond our
was here
and
let sky incubate
our footsteps
and
think
never
there –

wanted   still   always;

The Unsaid

autumned nights

know of
the
torn wrist
b
l
e
e
d
      ing
undercovers
the bloodshot eye
staring
      at the orangelit glow of
3 a.m.
of
rain and leaf

l   e   a   v   i   n g

left /gone/ severed/sentenced/sold/

of autumnednights of viagraed verses

versus

vers   us:

There Is No One (T)Here

mind cauterised
in
camouflage
rainwashed grass giving
respite
lips (always)
(lips)   always
silence and struggle
violence and silence
allowing
following
feeling
to

(be)   felt;
furious i hold the simplicity

f
a
l
l
i
n
g,

i fear the onset of next
and into out of within with insides like chalk circles carving
out a
language
spitting out a remembrance
holding onto the damage

to (heal)
lips (always)
lips always
ending in
sucked silence

(silence)
the silents;

Against (For My Children)

do not submit to the grey world
the grey world of grey faces in grey suits with greying thoughts
in greyed buildings of grey lives
do not allow your blue bluest bluer blue eyes cast grey looks
into
the beautiful wildness of your dreams
do not let the fake green their grey green
corrode your truth green
the green of fields of smiles of chlorophylled lips and
summerlicked meadows
do not let the greygreen gods of
envy lust money and greed
corrupt your mountainthoughts
your fieldvision and your rivereddreams
that
shall last forever
forever last
as long as your hearts shall
beat
beat
with the rainbowravaged song
of chromaed childhood belief

do not submit to their grey my loves

their grey ways my loves

my loves;

Nobodaddy

for clive payne & mark harris

*90% of all homeless and runaway children are from fatherless
homes and 60% of youth suicides are from fatherless homes*

tell us how we talk
tell us how we dress our children
tell us how much we have to pay you
tell us how pathetic a father we are
tell us how our children don't want to come with us
tell us what to buy them for christmas
tell us we are failures
tell us tell us   tell us
what time we have to pick up our children
the children we used to carry on our shoulders in timeless pride
and beautiful moments
the same children we have nurtured and fed awoke to their every
call and cry – bled our minds into total oblivion because of love
now we long now we stutter – afraid of your clocks your
prescription of behaviour your normality of objection
relinquish your entitlements dig your dogma as you destroy ours
as
now we walk head stooped watching through the cracks in the
playground wall –
now
you bastards
how dare you reduce us to nothings nothings
to a visitor a contact a saturday afternooned father a frightened
noun of crowned obsolescence
'be there at five
don't give them sweets
don't iron pyjamas

i wish you would hit me so that i could get an injunction
against
you
i regret the day i let them call you dad—'
dad   dad   dad;
we accuse
weaccuse
w   e   a   c   c   u   s   e
its time you listened –

*'the last time i spoke to my four-year-old daughter was 10 days
ago and it's been two months since i last saw her. I'd waited all
night for her to call. When it finally came, after chatting away
gaily for a few minutes she came out with the words ... daddy i
don't love you anymore'*
– clive payne on a recent phone call from his daughter in new
zealand.

*mark harris was imprisoned for 10 months for breaking a court
imposed order preventing him from seeing his children.*

Scardust

crawling to stand standing to crawl
crushed little fucker stuck to the sound
of a voice trapped underground
loving caring father hoping feeling son
why is it that you make my heart so fucked up
we
all alone face each day as wound
face each breath with anxiety no self-help book can cure
cannot speak cannot think everything inside curls and clings to
moments of meaning
to the insides dying to the beautiful selfsacrifice of
screaming –
the silence of silence the torment of torment the no of no
the knowing of knowing
so
run hide smile sleep
crushed little fucker don't get too deep
drowning in your aridity
thirsty in your ocean
cold in your climate
frightened of your comfort
holding onto your distance
dancing in your shadow
this loneliness i shall keep
and embroider it into my flesh
slit the throat to speak
place it in my thorax
crushed little fucker
remind myself i'm not to weep

screams find ears
in the loneliest of places
hearts heal
in empty spaces

One Million Blankets

one million blankets were given out during the kosovo conflict in
1999 the 6 billionth baby was recently born

to cover the world's pain
to warm the world's cold
to to to to
soak the world's blood
1 million blankets
shelter our frightened children
through the adulterated night
so put your hands beneath the covers
close your eyes
do not cry
for the tears freeze upon your lips
speak to the sky the beautiful breaking blue sky
above,
let the blanket shoulder the pain
let it drain
of all colours
flags emblems languages skins weapons anthems
onto
one flesh
undesignated uncountried deflagged and silent
yours and our flesh
one million blankets
in fields in mountains in doorways
in concrete
under the spiteful rain
beneath
the scorchingsun
upon the bloodsoaked snow
within

our atrophic hearts
these blankets know no borders
shelter stutters through words
words fucking words
can you hear them can you can you???

blanket bombing/blank it out/blanket bath/bloodblanket/
birthblanket/blanket of snow
blank out what you know
safety blanket/fire blanket/
your blanket/
my blanket our blanket
that covers our sins
indelible upon our skins
still they scream
scratched flesh no dreams
one million blankets
hide/safe/warm/clothe/care for/
this bloodless crucifixion
under the staring skies
that still sparkle
of sadness and despair

united by the blankets
yet torn by our language
lipped by our tongues
yet tortured because of our skins
one million blankets and 6 billion souls to save

one million blankets
but   it i s st   i 11   socoldhere

so cold here –

so cold,

so?

The In-Shining

children asleep
2 a.m.
in slowslumbered sanctity

no stitches to hold them together
no pills to help them sleep
no injections to detox their flesh
no flotation tanks to calm their minds
no health club vistas
no jogging machines
no heart rate testers
no lo cal handsfree go ahead it could be you maybe
sweetener free
low e
content
high fibre
traces of sodium
buy 1 get 2 points loyalty card mind manipulations

NO:

just these hands
these eyelids
under these stars
in
this breeze that blows
and this head
that hurts
trying to steady itself

bowing

before

      the candle stutters to sleep,

     to   sleep

Swan In Sunlight

for my mother

on mornings such as this
i wonder what it was like
when you were born
shone into this world like a sparkle
and
wonder how you played and ran
sang
and grew into
what made me

on mornings such as this
i see you in silent splendour
a swan in sunlight
swimming in slow water
against a green world
the feminisation
of my
masculinisation
the tears in the eye of man
the fist unfurling to
hold,
to hold   to hold

on mornings such as this
all i can do
is write my mind upon paper
to speak of things that truly matter
and
to acknowledge a life

of care   beauty
and motherhood hidden from heroes
on mornings such as this
i see you shine and sprinkle stars forever
a swan in sunlight

gliding
gliding
gliding......................

Sanctorum Number One

to james, monty and sue
july 2000

the flowers that grow
from the lips that cease
the todays that tear the throat
from tomorrow's speech
the space between
into
out of
within
within
the moments eternally melting
into the internalled resurrection
of yesterday
letters upon a stone
fragments of a life
prematurely torn
from this earthed desolation
still
still
too soon the knife
too late the words
wishing summer never came
wishing everything could be the same
and in the silent fields
the flowers that grow though the lips have ceased
in colour corroded chroma
stamen simplicity
of carvedcalm cacophony
in
this undying

grassgrowing
peace
in this
flowerfed silence
that speaks so eloquently
the flowers still grow
though the lips have ceased
the flowers still grow;
still
grow—

When We Wake Up Today
Will It Be Tomorrow?

evan jones, august 2000

will it
can it
ever
change
relinquish
free
to
be
ever
ever
to
ever
again
isn't
it
ever
ever?
if
we
can't
can
we
wake
up
ever
today,
tomorrow

Let Your Soul Start

ethan jones, 2001

icareformychildren
i wipe their cheeks
i cook them food
i smile at their jokes
i let them win
i always begin
i will not end
I am a dad
a father
unafraid to stand
in my falling
to be feminine
in my masculine
to be masculine in my masculine
i shall not bow my head
i shall not close my eyes
except to visualise my children
when they are away
then
but
now
i walk
head up to the wind
like trees stretching their chlorophylled necks to the sky
this sky my sky your sky

our sky

that will not die/that will not die

Delirium In White Silence

for rebekah and victoria

*In discussions about children's welfare [...] the term "parent" still
too easily becomes a synonym for "mother". Traditionally women
have been associated with the care and nurturance of children in
ways never expected of men. The term "mothering" [...] suggests a
warm protectiveness, a uniquely feminine form of affection. In
contrast, "fathering" implies only begetting* – Gittins, 1985

dragging itself from the hook
to parry suicidal thoughts
words blaze in unspokened arteries
resilience of moments
melting
only now
eternity stutters into the gap
the gap
that grows as it closes
don't know what to do – try to
busy myself with adult things
paint/ iron / read/ watch/ clean
when all i want to do is hear your voices in the room next door
all i want to do is wipe
your cheeks
all i want to do is tell you to be quiet –
pull your trousers up
tell you to eat your greens
and
and
and
and
wait for you to fall asleep

head wrapped against me
instead
i watch the red seconds tick
for hours
days
weeks
weak
am i?

it takes discipline to be this sad;

Such. Natural. Symmetry.

summer.park.sunlit.eyes.glint.
ending.day.opening.heart.
such.sky.such.souls.such togetherness.untorn.untimed.
wordsfromtonguesglide
like swifts in
summer.park.eyes.sunlit.me.watching.you.you.watching.me.us.
us

us

Commemoration And Amnesia

am i
an amnesiac
or a haemophiliac
or is this a heart attack?
that burns these holes in the lips
that shelters and stings
that blankets then burns
hurts and heals

to truth   to sadness
the   the
i devote
an increase in heartblood
to varnish and veneer
against their words that smear and snarl
i commemorate
i instigate
i must not fake
the this then why if how why and being
seeing feeling
crying of this silenced soul of tears and fears
that fall to stand
that fall to stand

how   i   remember
how   i   wish   to   forget

pathetic quimmo cripple bender poof girl

so i bottle your mind
with verbs that find
their place in nouns
of laced narcotic
underground
character disdenied
and undesigned and soul declined
i   bottle   your   mind
to commemorate
the pain this memory dawning
into   now
so know
so
no
and how i desecrate
to educate
and emancipate the chains that emaciate
the eyes that split my vision
the voices that stammered my tongue
yet now i speak
yet now i speak –
this war of attrition
this heartraged mission
this restricted code of breaking, breaking   recognition
am i
an amnesiac
or a haemophiliac
or
is this
a heart   attack –

Carelines

the ghosts of you make the spirit in me
footsteps fade
but nature grows
through the chlorophyll
my darkness diminishes
within this water
your reflection flows
within these trees
your liferings lip
this is the place
where peace exists
this is the place
where mind resists
the temptation to force
through this place
fracture fuses this is the place
where dirt is unsoiled
and time is the rustle of branches brattled and brown
the ghosts of you make the spirit in me
so go slow, inhabit the moment,
watch the meticulous melting ice upon frozen blade
river flow mind grow
delicate minutes spent tasting nothing
but the sky above and the earth below
the spirit of me makes the ghosts of you
live.

Let Being Be

alone on a mountain
early spring
thinking of who and what i am
alone, amongst
soaked earth brittled trees
burntblack grass
and how i am to be a father to my children
in this severance
this sacrifice of soul
that spits solitude into every corner and
here;
i fear i am an absent
a lostness concealed by wealth

i choke tears in supermarkets
hate people carriers
turn away from baby seats
buy crayons
tell the till operator my life story just to convince them i am a
parent
dream of tomorrow
but stay haunted by yesterday
and still
still these thoughts will not cease
they cascade like mountainpure water to some unknown yet
needed destination

these fragments i call mind
return
pecking at resilience
holing my hope

and here;
i swallow nature whole
trying to believe this must be it
there has to be a chance
a sky glint of somewhere starlight
that will burn holes into this darkness

and that the hands i made
will create me
that these fragments shall fuse a life
into fire
and that what i am
will let them be
who and what they wish to be

that all this pain this nocturnalled anxiety this waiting for
weekends to come and
that paul robeson robbie fowler the rock
christina rossetti jackson pollock
and a fragment of me
will somehow stay in their tinymassive minds

against this torrent called life we inhabit
and that somehow by going
i have never gone
only arrived at some cleaner point just like this water that rages
past me now
and that one day when they are men and women
that they may sit upon this mountain
under this sky
with calmed heart and
still
searching thoughts
and they may utter

the word father
with some semblance
of beauty
and recognition
and

know

know
that
they
they
are
un-alone

forever.

FROM

Against
(2003)

The War Is Dead Long Live The War

History repeats the mindicide
decade after decade
government after government
Lie after lie
Death after death

the war is dead long live the war

politics ignores the ordinary soul
in pursuit of power
greed oil and more
a sense of right and the need for wrong
forgetting the human death toll

the war is dead long live the war

faces change hatred don't
blind meat generals in camouflage suits
podium superstars for a moment
sidestepping lucidity
in the name of governmental fallacy perpetuation
policies scud themselves into homes
time after time after time after
while we honour the past avoid the present
and ignore the future

the war is dead long live the war
the war is dead long live

Final Score 1991

Out   of   this desert storm
War incursion newspeakstory briefings combat casual casualty
Capability cause effect death mess bullets misinformation maps
Men children women men media medical elucidation
Iraqi american brit bin laden bush enemy
Her hero soldier distance dispose impose gain loss
There here nowhere
The absolute sadness
Absolute absurdity
Absolute desolation
Absolute blindess
Absolute ignorance
Of
One
Human
Killing
Another.

Flag 2003

I shall create a new flag
Perhaps fly it from my home
I will first starve it of all colours
Then I shall amputate it of an anthem
Then when all is quiet I will murder its leader
Then cripple the government
And finally set fire to it
So it will never be able to fly
Then
I shall lay it upon the ground
For us to wipe our feet
Or
To stand on
For
We will always
See clearer
Further
If we
Climb
A little
H
  I
    G
      H
        E
               r/

Humanitas

we
begin standing up
by falling down
from suicide littered skies
in rope wrought regimes
a resilience

somewhere,
something meaningful
sometime,
nothing hurting
someone,
somewhere beautiful
some   where
everything being

somewhere

something meaningful

sometime

nothing hurting
someone
somewhere beautiful
somewhere
everything being,
being

FROM

Darkness Is Where The Stars Are
(2008)

Keys To Your Kingdom

for Reg Keys

*prince harry is back from afghanistan he flew out a twerp came
back a man. do you feel safer now he is back ... or should all the
royals be sent to iraq?* – Adrian Mitchell

privilege provides protection
from all the bombs and the hate
and affluence buys you abstention
from the battlefields of the occupied state

an accident of birth or
a victim of geography
the rules are not the same
for soldiers Keys, Tom and wales windsor, prince harry

it is strange how harry's father and grandfather
parade like pariahs on Poppy Day
drenched in medals
splattered in ribbons like stapled cadavers

as,
Tom's father, only wears one,
the face of his murdered son,
where no tomorrows grow, today
as the holes gape like a cenotaph sunday

so, pride is indifferent to suffering
and suffering must be for the chosen
or so we are told
or led to believe in history lessons
in a coalition of the willing
it is only those chosen, ripe for the killing

oh Wilfred your words
stick in my throat
100 years ago you wrote
'*pro patria mori*, the old lie'   their   old   lie
you warned us yet no one heard
and your words drifted like ash in the november sky
as now, today, still,
young men and women are sent to another trench
in another country
for another man's pride
to fight another man's war
but
only if you don't matter
to the country you're fighting for.

Shadowboxing

I place the suitcase upon the bed,as before,I unzip,as before,I
pack,first the dettol stung cheeks flu hot hidden holes,held, then
the confusion,head spun days clinging to tomorrow and the
child's bedtime story – a respite escape.The hollow head of
spent tears,torn,sunlight shreds the room as I push the bibles
deep within,fade,as memory burns gaps in the ice,I blink,
knowing the unknown, again, again, again.Sediment of carcass
devours coherence and I shiver,cease to be, feel then choke my
now, again, as before. I find the Christmas you stole my inno-
cence, crushed fairy wings sleep within, pour the unopened
wine, sweep the crumbs away...away. Drench yesterdays
in blood, 'submit' you screamed, how could I when I had no-
thing to give up.Uneven days and insomnia slow night
s.Hold.Hold still, focus, gone, be there, gone, be there, safe,
shaking recollected in safety, slow,inhale,heal,here, here, heal
hear? Your perfume your halitosed tongue, your jewels the
thorns of briar bush, your make-up my blood on your
lip,bury.....Bury in the suitcase cave,breathe, breathe, close the
door open the curtains, feel the sunlight upon my
face,.........Zip, packed,..........As before yet this time, I open the
curtains, go go going go ,feel the sunlight upon my face,suck
cool air in liberated lungs, zipped, packed, of you, you
you,no
trace, no   trace,

Dandelion

from the mouths of corpses
the seeds shall fly
into inside
the ocean is
like weeds eclipsed by flower suns
light will stutter through
wait and watch
the epiphany said
collapse and start again
be a companion to isolation
a friend of regret
a slow breeze blowing through time
a child's breath can mend our sight

the starting clocks of unending daylight
so lay down in seed dawn
away from the deep cut night
the inherent beauty of our scattered souls
searching sacred earth for another place
as
with these holes we become whole

so
fly   fly   fly   away
what we have been is what we are
mother of millions fathers of forever
fly   fly   fly   away
into   the   inside
as
what breaks, shall become
for
we are the traces

the traces
left for the next

the next,

the

In Absentia

i light a candle for the absents
the almost forgotten, the waiting, the worn
a day light for the dark nights
a filament of throat from thought
i light a candle for the absents
the disappeared, the frightened,
the watching, the saturday fathers,
disneyland dads, happy meal patriachs,
contact controlled, access asked
permission prayered
the deadbeat, child support agents
no rights only deepest responsibility
i stare into the flame
see love and hate
unite
in
one
silent flicker
a black and white photograph in a golden frame

but

from the slit wrist
the rose will grow
from the distance
blazes the geography of the soul
like candles, we inhabit the night
absence is not abstention
what feeds the wick?
who starves the oxygen?
and
what child is not made from woman and man?

Dialogues With The Deaf

for my grandfather Stanley Jones and great grandfather
George Stockdale

in the calm safety of my radiatored room
my freshly washed hand clicks at the white mouse,
tips of fingers tap tenderly at the letters
the quiet comforting hum of the computer screen
i dig into history
like the speed of memory
i find the site
commonwealth war graves commission
the years flash like teeth in front of me
i find the link to 'the dead of world war 1'
like an afterthought
like an ebay helpline
i type in my mother's grandfather's name
two words that give flesh to this plastic
two words that have been
two words that lived and breathed,
loading, loading
my mobile rings, i ignore
i find the reference
then pay by code and credit card
for his medal card
then
it is delivered silently through an invisible universe
and my breathing jars, my hands sweaty
screaming like a star
shot like a spear through the years
the mustard gas tears
the mud soaked trenches, the hysterical yelping,
the blood, the bleeding, amputations, destruction,

sludge drudge and victorious speeches
a battered white and black photograph
of a medal record
two words,
this time amongst millions
two words of hope
and pride
i check the details
yes, that's him
two words amongst history's narrative
i try to imagine his face, his eyes staring at the fields,
his fingertips blacked and gnarled, his boots
his tin mug, his pencil letters
his waiting to return home
i read the card
theatre of war
france
applause, audience, entertainment   theatre?
then scribbled like a child's handwriting

'Dead'

all those years, filed away in some grey building
sleeping next to a million other 'Dead' souls
unknown, unseen, unheard of
un

i save the photograph in my file
knowing i must never lose this document
turn off the computer
face the empty screen
face myself
turn away from history
face the future

The Love Of Blood

Will
Fail
Will eventually haemorrhage
Fed by ignorance
Will fade
If blood is our god
To belong is not to bleed
But congeal like putrid jelly
In the failing of flowing
Is the avoidance of knowing
Not that soul that is nothing
And how your blood is nothing
Nothing but a biological necessity
Love your blood and you shall bleed
The blood of hatred fear oppression
Blood out of pain concealed
But
The blood of love shall outlast your love of blood
For belonging is not a dna code
The blood of love
Flows/ knows/ is / will be
healing sealing seeking increasing
never harming or desecrating
and the blood of love
shall rise and overflow
and knows
that belonging is not where you come from but what
you   are at
shall multiply
drowning
the love of blood
until
it bleeds
into knowledge not judgement

Conflict Tactics Scale

Shut the door
Put out the light
Dream of yesterday
but keep everything out of sight
first the silence
the atrophic acts of attention seeking
then the questions,
from the foamfrothed mouth of power and control
then the eyes
stone stare of storm electric
my home a cage
I cannot escape
Only endure for the sake of my children
And their need for safety

Scared to answer the phone
In case it is my mother
So sit in stomach cramped stasis
As you isolate my identity
And feed it to your insecurity
Because I am a nobody a shit a fake a runt cunt
loser nothing mummy's boy mummy's boy
a doll with a penis a sexless mannequin
a father, a man, a human?
Yet I am everyone
Who ever felt
The nails in the cheek
Their lives patrolled
Their minds controlled
The kick down the stairs
The stinging slap on anxious skin
The belittling tongue of torpid torture

That never sleeps
Just waits at my side
For the wounds to bleed
Then licks and licks until
I can no longer heal
So limp
Fat bloated belly, passive receptor
Of all your hatred
Then crawl
Crushed beetle
On all fours, to the door, an escape
But
Stop
And listen,
Hear my child's cry
'Dad, Dad, Dad—'
he's caught his finger in his bedroom door
I stand up, breathe
Blank out your noise
Cradle his warm body
I close the door
Put out the light
Wait for tomorrow
But
Keep   everything   out   of   sight.

FROM

The Aspirations Of Poverty
(2017)

The proletarians have nothing to lose but their chains.
They have a world to win.

– The Communist Manifesto

The Aspirations Of Poverty

Poverty of aspiration is what keeps people poor – Janet Daley

Say what you believe
Believe what you say
– Tony Benn

I did not vote for trident
for library closures or the bedroom tax
I would have rather crossed out
PIP reviews, benefit cuts and zero hour contracts
Rees-Mogg's expenses and Johnson's pranks
But now it appears
I support the repeal of the anti hunting bill
and scrapping the human rights act
I can't remember agreeing
to trickledown economics
where food banks spiral
as do corporate profits
because this is the age of selfeconomics
a paranoid mathematics
of all against all

I didn't buy in
to the great NHS sell off
or to have my streets
overseen by G4SS
And I certainly didn't vote for
letting in foreigners
(only rich ones of course)
because of TTIP
The transatlantic trade and investment partnership
a tory policy gangbang is there ever was one
an assault on democracy

amputate national sovereignty
and guaranteed hardship
with the mantra of free. Market e. con. Omy
ignoring fairness and equality
though I would let in the asylum seeker
who's faced death in their own country
on this I agree
I don't remember signing my soul away
for a snooper's charter instead of free speech
I wanted all over each
every not one
solidarity instead of solitary
equality of opportunity
not nepotistic minority
I make doors
not build walls
believe in sharing
not gathering shares
all this greed
has left a gaping need
in giving not just taking

educating not desecrating
in living, breathing,
not hiding, stealing wheeling dealing
I believe in stoic steadfast articulacy
speaking out against
this created culture of austerity
a searing eloquent vocabulary
to match this capricious cretin confederacy
their 'we're all in this together big society'
doublespeak conspiracy
in the name of progression
they sell us termination
as wedding parades mask the charade

of the emancipation masquerade
we're in fiscal atrophy
while they declare another bankruptcy
But, I, me you us
We

because I do believe
there IS such a thing as society
and I, we, are willing to help build it
so fuck your deficit
you made it
are the main culprit
so you fix it
because we we are not your passive puppets
because we we believe in something more
than a blossoming city portfolio
something more fulfilling
than going solo

and as you preach from your poisoned pulpit
the grasping gospel of planned poverty
your master and servant ideology
we aim to connect, organise, act
and attempt to find it
we will not be your scapegoats
for your policy, cutthroat
our lives shall be exalted
our community devoted
From Aberfan to Orgreave
Hillsborough to Grenfell
like the figures in a battered Lowry
not to treat human life as mere commodity
as these, these
are my aspirations that arise
from   my, my   poverty

In The Garden of Power and Control

The
Gardener
Stalks and walks the paths,
Edging escape
And cutting strays
Epiphany of control and
Dedication to duty
Ultimately
Their spades
Consume all beauty

That does not fit into the correct
Scheme of things
I bloom on a postage stamp lawn
A requiem for a field
That somewhere once sang
Cut and cropped, lulled and dulled
Into R e s e r v a tion
I relinquish my redwood dreams
For a pruned and cleaned
Bonsai in a pot
My colour, corroded
My stem, hewn
My leaves, turned upside down
Only artificial sun slithers through
As all I see
Is the polished gleam of the gardener's boots
My sap spills
My light lost
My roots stuck fast to soil
Wait wait for a change of shift
So drift in delirium of love

Over the wall
It's funny how a lover plants their seeds......

The Healing House

bring your children to the nursery
with their disease and sickness,
this is the place where I hope to cure all illness
at the point of need, this is an emergency

come now, our tomorrow
rest yourself
as i halt fear and heal bone marrow,
and, from an early death
i promise emancipation,
with my doctors, nurses
and vaccinations

let in the mothers
the pool is ready for another,
carer of the next generation,
sleep, prepare for this new birth,
I offer you protection,
as you grow the roots of our new earth

welcome, people from other nations,
with troubled faces from distant places,
i have room for you, my new patients,
i have no borders to caring,
pain has no dialect, this language is for sharing
let love be found in translation

sit, eat from my pantry,
become healthy
as you, you are my ultimate test,
bring me your tortured tongues
so you may speak again
from far off battlefields show your scarred flesh
so i can stem the blood and heal your pain.

to you, the wiser, the elderly, the old,
do not be afraid, do not huddle in the cold,
my door is open,
come in, come in,
it is warm, trust us,
and i shall lance the boils of poverty's injustice,
and drain the infection,
as in my house these rooms
offer cure by prevention,

and so to the sick, to the dying, those crippled with
disease
stay, in my garden,
breath,
lay, beneath the trees
i shall provide peace and serenity
to strengthen the health of vulnerability
no matter what age, sex, class, race or country,

my windows pour penicillin
my library, the words of the masters,
Simpson, Pasteur and Fleming
not market forces or ignorant capitalists

so be careful how you treat your house, our home
never neglect or leave alone
keep clean, add extensions
but never damage the bricks or remove my foundations

183

from the wasteland of squalor, disease and
dereliction,
I am the safe place
the healing home
injecting cells with reconstruction,
the everlasting bandage
to deliver all from illnessed bondage
I am the suture
to stitch the wounds of the past
but i am the scalpel
to carve the future
to make this dream last
to make this dream last.

Shed, Valley, Life

the verb is more important than the noun – Aneurin Bevan

Patterns of years
Etched
Into wooden throats
Of scars
And other wars,
Fought,
Thought
By summer swift twilight
Oil spilled
Worn like a suit
And
Tilled
Until sleep
Tiled floor with leftovers from bathroom in 1983
Holy jam jars
Burst with metallic manfruit
Screws decoded by size, flat head or Phillips
Nails waiting for their turn for glory
Saved, picked up, never bought, martyred
From skip passings
And floorboard torture,
Man needs no god
When he has a hammer
A saw
And a half empty tub of swarfega
Just time,
Captured in a frozen vice
Radio fizz
And cricketed summerswallows
Of botham and jeff thompsons

Only ashes
Only ashes
Still burn, burnt, burns
A hundred cricket bats
Glued, hewn, smoothed
And saved for another day
A thousand punctures
Bubbled, bottled and bandaged
hope labelled, love tidied, freedom captured and safety nailed
I never quite knew what to do in this, my father's room,
I think i do now,
Shed, shed

It Will Take More Than A Grave To Bury You

To Commemorate the Senghenydd Mine Disaster of 1913

like the mountain stream carving its way to the sea
like the root underground made up of you and me
through the shadows of the night
flickers return of their forgotten light

it will take more than a grave to bury you
it will take more than death for us to forget you
it will take more than a grave to bury you
like candles burning alone
their voices are what brings us home

what sweet songs spilled themselves upon our tongues
back to when our world was still so young
what memories mesmerised
our fading eyes under cobalt skies

it will take more than a grave to bury you
it will take more than death for us to forget you
it will take more than a grave to bury you
like candles burning alone
their voices are what brings us home

it will take more than death for us to forget you
like candles burning alone
their voices are what brings us home

it will take more than a grave to bury you

Life Exi(S)Ts

down the blue highways of their minds
the group at Pentre House nursing home
take me
into the hidden fields of chroma symphonies
over desert wars
between terraced streets of home
and
the teacher who would slap their faces
if they got an answer wrong

each
wait patiently
for their turn to speak
to take me on a gentle hazy walk down a troubledtough life,
I see blackouts
and mountain hideouts
odd shoes
and balanced morals
glittering moments
stoic as stones
simple as grass
visionary
through fading sight,
a recollection
of that last dance,

'we interrupt this poem to tell you that the royal baby is going
to be called,
george'

why
not commemorate
and celebrate
before its too late,

why
not park cameras, stepladders
sky reporters
nicholas fucking witchell.
Outside
the nursing homes
to capture their speeches
their tinymassive triumphs
their stuttered elegies
of worked-class dignity
and
today 'Muriel Evans gave birth
to the most beautiful hair do this morning,
it's been a long wait,
but its done
sprayed to perfection,
held to the light
she's almost a film star
and here's Dennis Jones, 93 years old,
stick in hand,
on his way
to vote'

not
this mannequin parade
of pensionned parasites
that expect a curtsey

not
these etoneducated
nepotisticnothings
waving from a balcony

not this
mediocre idiocracy
craving
messianic authority

no,
tell me about 1926
when you had soup and bread at the local chapel
tell me of
how the women of Senghenydd
helped raise £120 thousand for the relief fund
when the mine owners got fined £24
tell me tell me
lead me
through this darkness
to a place
where sunlight broke through the clouds

make me laugh when you recount how your
brother was locked in a school cupboard
by his teacher for urinating over
his tormentors who called him 'welsh rarebit'
make me cry
as you tell me how your mother died when
you were four months old and your older sister
brought you and your 10 siblings up
make me think
when you tell me
of your survival techniques

and
the blue highways
ramble on,
ravaged by time
yet strengthened by struggle
littered by death
but overflowing with life

the doors are open
but they've already gone

life exits

life
life exists,
in life exits

Driftwood (Lives)

for alan, galip and rehan kurdi

just coming from one of those countries does not make you a genuine asylum seeker – nigel farage

if we allow all who come in leaky boats to stay, then more will come in leaky boats – david davies mp

cast out
washed up
spat upon
from an indifferent land
splintered lives
dream of rebuilding tomorrow
sail away
doors from walls
peace from sorrow

hammered
nailed
trapped
in airless holds
beneath the endless blue sky
holding on, holding on

from space the oceans span like birdflight
but in the coal black emptiness
manacles are served
as the water swallows the detritus of a dream
like plankton

they walk the plank
they walk the plank

as all inclusive holidays are enjoyed and
all ucaneat buffets are gorged
and azure swimming pool selfies
shared on facebook
tiny mouths
ingest salt water
and fall into black unconsciousness
so unprepared to die

drift drift
look away look away
our borders protect us from this
our borders legitimise this
as the waves bring in
what the world discarded
returning ideals to
the unforgiving land

polka dot dresses and
fresh nappies
washed up on the sand
tidewracked and soulwracked

a mutiny of mankind
this trembling timber of thoughtstabbing thoughtlessness

a black parade of would be coffins
drift
onto deserted holidaymade beaches
the headline says 'migrants'
i see women men and children

owing to a well-founded fear of being persecuted for reasons of race,
religion, nationality, membership of a particular social group or
political opinion, is outside the country of their nationality, and is
unable to, or owing to such fear, is unwilling to avail themselves of
the protection of that country.

in other words

refugees
in other words
our common humanity
you and me

the flotsam of humanity
washed up
cast out
skintides of sadness

perhaps

a kind of kindling

to set fire
to ignorance and a p a thy

FROM

My Bright Shadow
(2020)

In The Words Of Men

since you passed,
Mother,
dad and i sometimes
don't know what to say
after the platitudes
stuttered attempts to comfort
'take each day as it comes'
there is a screaming slow silence
that drowns our tongues,
not like the silence of trees in the blue breeze
but an arms open
aching quiet of the wilderness
so,
i've taken to
talking
of my hoped for, yet imaginary
diy projects;
building a garden fence,
skirting board replacement,
b&q excursions
and the grout,
always the grout.

suddenly,
his voice grows enthused,
transported to hands on reality
a muscled memory
blanket
that,
for a moment,
wraps us in a safe place
and

the way
a dovetail joint
brings two separated pieces together,
or
how sanding with the grain
makes for smoother staining
and of course,
vacuum before
grouting
to give a better, cleaner,
more lasting
fix,
picks us up from the floor
and we walk again
to the next job,
Mam,

The Smell Of Sundays

especially the afternoons,
my Mother, ironing
listening to the radio,
the archers omnibus or football
steamed up windows
fragments of security stored,
delicately
supremely
safety framed in the freshly folded jumper
waiting for the panic of morose monday mornings
and the drumming dread of
double maths and simultaneous equations,
no,
not
yet,
just the roar of the crowd
on the radio as the ball hits the net,
and
the smoothness of cotton sheets
the hiss and swirl of steam,
this contraband of hope
and
my
Mother's hands
ironing
out
the
creases,   for now

Wrapped In The Arms Of Ghosts

like us all craving meaning
who live and have lived
death encircles us
the dying embalm our breathing

comfort or carrion
bandage or burying
the leaving or the carrying

clinging to sepia stained memories
bleeding frames and flickering effigies
hearing voices from forgotten melodies
is yesterday to be our only legacy

cradle me with your smile
deliver us
when it's time
let this
tearblind iris
give me sight
when all i can see
is
the searing daylight

you are tourniquet
when i am wound
you are the stilling voice
if i lose my sound

when the litany of disaffection
plays in my head
you are the chorus of resurrection

reminding me of what
i need to transcend

comfort or carrion
bandage or burying
the leaving or the carrying
wrapped in the arms of our ghosts
wandering in the mists of our innermost
safe in the knowledge of the betrothed
it is with you that i am clothed

Lovesung

catkin, primrose, cherry plum
pussy willow
today i got so tired of
bullets, stabbings, trump and
hashtag 'this'
i looked outside
my window
and saw that the sun was shining
and blue was in the air
a shimmering wintered light
held all things new
so i opened my mouth and spoke of you
catkin, primrose, cherry plum
pussy willow
the faded winter colours
carrying tomorrow
in their today
asking nothing
offering everything
freedom sits on the frozen branch
a bud not a gun,
a begun
not an undone,

catkin, primrose,
pussy willow,
cherry plum,
and
somewhere
a   bird   is   singing

At St Non's Well

where edge clings to air
as a baby's hand reaches for love,
a
star sun showers winter
with warmth,
where waves batter rocks
send white spray glittering to blue

is this the well we drink from?
is this the silent spring that shudders
the tiny trickles
rivulets of remembrance
floods,
of love
letting loss
untie itself
and spill to the sucking sea
timetorn tears
wash the want away
mudmanacled fears
unleashed and unbounded
free,
now,
enough,
to say,
a river of memoria
umbilical to the sea,
tourniquet of hope,
milk of millennia
flowing expectantly
to where the
blind find the sight

the stammer meets eloquence
the scream,
the silence,
and the imprisoned rise
to transcendence

hold,
hold still
still hold
the sea sown seeds of imagination
from the cracks of dislocation
swim now,
drink now
hear then,
for   when.

Come Back, Mother

i sense a slipping back,
away from,
overnight
a notthereness
your beautiful face
filled with worrylines
a going
a wall
a   wan   d   er
  in

          g
i try to hold you back
stroke your hand
smooth your forehead
iron out the frowns
as once you did to my creases
but   there is   a   g   a   p
i cannot see
but feel
as if you
are becoming your own Mother
your skin so thin
a fading polaroid
a translucent awning
protecting,
a topography of you,
sweet Mother,
irene
peace, peace
but you have none today,
a silent mantra
offers itself to the world
Mother, come back,
come back, Mother

The Gutting Of Grief

plunder this heart
drag me to the edge
drain me out
distil every last drop of blood   into drought
excoriate each atom   of this failing flesh

o plunder this heart
for i shall embroider loss   into my arteries
i shall weave this whittling war   across my throat
and wear it like a shawl
i shall strip myself   down to the bared bones
humility   shall guide my   arrogance

for i do not matter
yet i embody all that matters

i shall be humus
which means – of the earth –
and the rocks and crags lakes and streams
stones and shores   shall carry me
that starlight
that breaks through my darkness
is also
your light/ crucified/ and risen
i shall breathe to the deepest core
of this molten orb
floating
in the cataclysm of space
and solder sorrow onto soul
i suck the spirits of those
who have passed before me
i wander in their detritus

dreaming their details
piecing together
the fragments of vanished moments
life from the lives
love from the loving

i am inside of myself
from the outsideness

plunder this heart if you must
i let this gutting grief
become a river through me
not a dam,
it is in suffering
that i trust
it shall surge and fill
for it to leave me
but i cannot predict
that exit
i have to become the entrance
and the release
to rise in its rising
to fall under its weight
as when
the stomach somersaults in sorrow
my fingers shake in adrenalised weakness
and my tears burn holes in my eyelids
that i know
i know
that i have lived
that i have loved,
for grief is the cipher
to pinpoint our acute awareness
from the scorching sun of despair

and to say,
i have witnessed
a life,
i was there
i have walked that precipice
almost been blinded
at the sight
but but but
in that fleeting flash
that flutter of fury
lived and lives
an eternalling light
that shall sit within our darkness
living,
beating on
brightening the shadows

i have lived in the grip of grief
which could only have been
birthed from such sad sweetness
in losing we become all that we once
resisted

for we do not matter
yet we embody all that matters

so plunder this heart

for then
        I know
                it will at least have existed,

FROM

Even in Exile
(2020)

Recuerda

Recuerda when they come to your door
With their laws and their guns
When they take your daughters
And lead away your sons
Recuerda Thatcher Nixon Pinochet
How the land of the free
Disappeared those who would not obey
In the name of liberty

What was once lost
We will find again
What is true will
Will always transcend

Cofiwch when they drowned a community
When they buried a school
When they silenced a language
When there's so much to lose
Songs that welcome
Songs that warn
For a future
That is yet to be born
Recuerda
Remember
Recuerda
Remember

Thirty Thousand Milk Bottles

Thirty thousand bottles
In a generation's hands
Holding hope consistent
Clutching cold nourishment
Thirty thousand bottles
In a generation's hands
Thirty thousand milk bottles
For this is our demand

Thirty thousand bottles
Shall remember the love
Pouring back justice
From all that was culled
Reclaiming lives from the damned
For this is our land
For this is our land

Thirty thousand bottles
One for each lonely death
They must not be in vain for the memory of the dispossessed
Thirty thousand bottles
They must not be in vain
Forever they shall
They shall remain

Thirty thousand bottles
Building beliefs and bones
A shared understanding
Beneath their gilded thrones
Thirty thousand bottles
In a generation's hands
Thirty thousand milk bottles
For this is our demand

Thirty thousand bottles
Shall remember the love
Pouring back justice
From all that was culled
Reclaiming lives from the damned
For this is our land
For this is our land

Thirty thousand bottles
One for each lonely death
They must not be in vain for the memory of the dispossessed
Thirty thousand bottles
They must not be in vain
Forever they shall
They shall remain

The Last Song

Bondaged citizens
Make the best revolutions
Asking questions
The deepest answer
The blood paints our protest

Untie the noose
Here is the ladder
One step at a time
Be unafraid to climb
They took your hands
But they could not silence your tongue
The darkest night
The last song

So the wounds purify
Our purpose to unify
We fall between
Dialects and time
Like pilgrims we will find

Untie the noose
Here is the ladder
One step at a time
Be unafraid to climb
They took your hands
But they could not silence your tongue
The darkest night
The last song

Notes

Epigraphs: '…it does not matter/ to be one more stone, the dark stone,/ the pure stone which the river bears away' is taken from Pablo Neruda's poem 'Oh Earth, Wait for Me'. 'Whoever you are, no matter how lonely, the world offers itself to your imagination,' is taken from Mary Oliver's poem 'Wild Geese'. 'The proletarians have nothing to lose but their chains. They have a world to win.' is taken from *The Communist Manifesto*, Karl Marx and Friedrich Engels (1848).

The Penis Prayer: The epigraph is taken from the BBC interview with Emily Maitlis in 2019.

A Little Patience: All capitals are Gary Barlow or Take That songs

Trawsblaniad Enaid/ Soul Transplant/ Ruh Zara'Aa: 'These don't look like children to me – We should do dental testing to certify the age of refugees' is a comment made in 2016 by Tory Monmouth MP David Davies and is a position which he defended, as reported by news.sky.com, on Thursday 20 October 2016 (https://news.sky.com/story/mp-calls-for-child-migrant-tooth-age-checks-10623262, accessed 11/08/2021). 'There are no borders in space' is a quote from Nasa spacefarer Mikhail Kornienko of the Russian space agency Roscosmos as he prepared to start his year-long tenure on the International Space Station, as reported by newscientist.com (https://www.newscientist.com/article/mg22630210-700-martian-magna-carta-justice-and-freedom-on-the-final-frontier /, accessed 11/08/2021).

To Be Or Not: The James Baldwin quote is from an extensive 1963 profile interview with LIFE magazine in the May 24 issue. Written by Jane Howard, this quote is taken from a section about empathy and reading and went on to say: 'It was Dostoevsky and Dickens who taught me that the things that tormented me most were the very things that connected me with all the people who were alive, or who ever had been alive. Only if we face these open wounds in ourselves can we understand them in other people.'

This poem is based on the first and last words of these life changing books and poems that many pupils will now never read:

1984	George Orwell
The Waste Land	T S Eliot
The Handmaid's Tale	Margaret Atwood
I Know Why The Caged Bird Sings	Maya Angelou
A Clockwork Orange	Anthony Burgess

Reeva Steenkamp and Me was written in response to the *Dear Christine* exhibition curated by Fionn Wilson.

Where The Songs Come From: 'Until the middle Pleistocene Britain was a peninsula of Europe, connected by a massive chalk anticline, the Weald-Artois Anticline across the Straits of Dover' (https://en.wikipedia.org/wiki/Doggerland, accessed 8/7/2021).

Gwrandewch/Listen: 'Hazrem Hazardous Waste Recycling Plant is built in Cwmfelinfach in 2021. It will emit 20,000 tonnes of Carbon Dioxide into the atmosphere every year' (http://www.democracy.caerphilly.gov.uk/documents/s33703/ Code%20No%2020%200806%20NCC%20Land%20At%20

Grid%20Ref%20319235%20191320%20Nine%20Mile%20 Point%20Ind%20Estate%20-%20Report.pdf, accessed 11/8/2021). Irene Jones, Patrick's mother, was at the forefront of a campaign to save St David's Wood when the Blackwood bypass was built.

Ord Fest: Ord Fest is Swedish for word feast.

Their Life On Their Heads: The epigraph is from the newspaper article 'Lonely death in a crowded cornfield' written by Julian Borger, *The Guardian*, 15 July 1995.

Demonstrations For Existence: The Aneurin Bevan quote is from a 1952 speech.

Nobodaddy: '90% of all homeless and runaway children are form fatherless homes and 60% of youth suicides are from fatherless homes' – The National Center for Fathering (www.fathers.com/statistics-and-research/the-extent-of-fatherlessness/, accessed 11/8/2021).

Delirium In White Silence: The Gittins quote is taken from Diana Gittins, *The Family in Question: Changing Households and Familiar Ideologies*, Macmillan, Basingstoke, 1985.

Keys To Your Kingdom: The epigraph is taken from the Adrian Mitchell poem 'Prince Harry in Afghanistan'.

The Aspirations Of Poverty: 'Poverty of aspiration is what keeps people poor' is an article written for *the Telegraph* by Janet Daley in August 2002 (https://www.telegraph.co.uk/comment/personal-view/3580964/Poverty-of-aspiration-is-what-keeps-people-poor.html, accessed 11/8/2021).

It Will Take More Than A Grave To Bury You: 439 men and boys killed; 542 children left fatherless; 200 widows. The mine owners were fined £24. 1 shilling and a penny farthing for each life. £126,000 was collected by The Disaster Relief Fund and by 1951 over £195,000 had been distributed. King George did not visit the village as he was attending the marriage of Prince Arthur and Princess Alexandra.

Driftwood (Lives): The 1951 Refugee Convention defines a refugee as: 'someone who is unable or unwilling to return to their country of origin owing to a well-founded fear of being persecuted for reasons of race, religion, nationality, membership of a particular social group, or political opinion.'

Acknowledgements

Poems appear from *Darkness is Where the Stars Are* (Cinnamon Press, 2008), *The Aspirations of Poverty* (Red Poets Press, 2017) and *My Bright Shadow* (Rough Trade Books, 2020) with the kind permission of their publishers.

Lyrics appear from James Dean Bradfield's album *Even in Exile* (2020) with kind permission from BMG Music Publishing, 2020.

From the new poems, 'You' was first published in *Poetry Wales* in 2020; 'Fucking Echoes' was published in *The Lonely Crowd* in 2019; 'The Aspirations of Poverty' and 'Demonise or Die' appeared on *Renegade Psalms* with John Robb (Louder Than War Records) in 2019.

Thanks to Matilda Joon, Susie Wildsmith, Richard Davies, James Dean Bradfield, Nicholas Jones, John Robb, Iqroop Chopra, Rhys Mwyn and Trevor Jones.

PARTHIAN *Poetry in Translation*

Home on the Move
Two poems go on a journey
Edited by Manuela Perteghella
and Ricarda Vidal
ISBN 978-1-912681-46-4
£8.99 | Paperback
'One of the most inventive and necessary
poetry projects of recent years…'
– Chris McCabe

Pomegranate Garden
A selection of poems by Haydar Ergülen
Edited by Mel Kenne, Saliha Paker
and Caroline Stockford
ISBN 978-1-912681-42-6
£8.99 | Paperback
'A major poet who rises from [his] roots to touch
on what is human at its most stripped-down,
vulnerable and universal…'
– Michel Cassir, *L'Harmattan*

Modern Bengali Poetry
Desire for Fire
Arunava Sinha
ISBN 978-1-912681-22-8
£11.99 | Paperback
This volume celebrates over one hundred years
of poetry from the two Bengals represented
by over fifty different poets.

PARTHIAN *Poetry*

Hey Bert
Roberto Pastore
ISBN 978-1-912109-34-0
£9.00 | Paperback
'Bert's writing, quite simply, makes me happy.
Jealous but happy.'
– Crystal Jeans

Sliced Tongue and Pearl Cufflinks
Kittie Belltree
ISBN 978-1-912681-14-3
£9.00 | Paperback
'By turns witty and sophisticated, her writing shivers
with a suggestion of unease that is compelling.'
– Samantha Wynne-Rhydderch

Hymns Ancient & Modern
New & Selected Poems
J. Brookes
ISBN 978-1-912681-33-4
£9.99 | Paperback
'It's a skilful writer indeed who can combine elements both
heartbreaking and hilarious: Brookes is that writer.'
– Robert Minhinnick

How to Carry Fire
Christina Thatcher
ISBN 978-1-912681-48-8
£9.00 | Paperback
'A dazzling array of poems both remarkable in their ingenuity,
and raw, unforgettable honesty.'
– Helen Calcutt

PARTHIAN *Poetry*

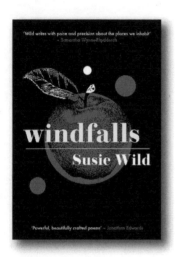

Windfalls

SUSIE WILD
ISBN 978-1-912681-75-4
£9.00 • Paperback

'Powerful, beautifully crafted poems...
there's nothing like poetry to cut down
the spaces between us, to leap across gaps,
make a friend of a stranger.'
– Jonathan Edwards

Small

NATALIE ANN HOLBOROW
ISBN 978-1-912681-76-1
£9.99 • Paperback

'Shoot for the moon? Holborow has landed,
roamed its face, dipped into the craters, and
gathered an armful of stars
while up there.'
– Wales Arts Review

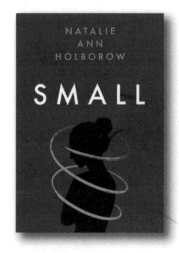